MEASURING NOMINAL AND EFFECTIVE PROTECTION

to my mother

to the memory of my father

Measuring Nominal and Effective Protection:

The Case of Mexico

ADRIAAN TEN KATE
Erasmus University
Rotterdam

Avebury

Aldershot · Brookfield USA · Hong Kong · Singapore · Sydney

Published by

Avebury

Gower Publishing Company Limited
Gower House
Croft Road
Aldershot
Hants GU11 3HR
England

Gower Publishing Company
Old Post Road
Brookfield
Vermont 05036
USA

ISBN 0 566 05239 3

Printed in Great Britain by
Richard Clay Ltd, Bungay, Suffolk.

Contents

List of tables and diagrams   viii

Preface   x

1. Introduction

1.1 Purpose and Scope of the Study   1

1.2 Outline of the Contents   2

1.3 Contribution of the Study   4

2. Conceptual Framework

2.1 Assessing the Effects of Economic Policy   7

2.2 Foreign-Trade Regimes   8

2.3 Free Trade   9

2.4 Systems of Protection   10

2.5 Indirect Taxes under Free Trade   12

2.6 Price Control under Free Trade   14

2.7 Free-Trade Conditions   15

2.8 Free-Trade Situation   16

3. Nominal Protection

3.1 Background   18

3.2 The Nominal Rate of Protection of a Product 20

3.3 Assumptions Underlying the Estimation of
    Free-Trade Prices   22

3.4 Ordinary Versus Net Nominal Protective Rates 27

3.5 The Nominal Protective Rate of a Basket of
    Products   29

v

4. Measuring Nominal Protection

4.1 Measuring Nominal Protection Through Tariffs   33

4.2 Measuring Nominal Protection Through Price
    Comparison   43

4.3 Combining the Price Comparison Approach with
    the Tariff Approach   50

5. Effective Protection

5.1 The Effective Rate of Protection   57

5.2 Estimating the Value Added at Free-Trade Prices   60

5.3 Input-Output Calculations of Effective
    Protection   68

5.4 Implications   78

5.5 Numerical Example   81

6. Non-Tradable Goods and Services

6.1 Introductory Remarks   89

6.2 Assumptions Regarding the Price Response of
    the Non-Tradables   93

6.3 Incorporating Non-Tradable Inputs in the
    Value-Added   99

6.4 Contribution of Non-Tradable Inputs to
    Effective Protection   104

6.5 Concluding Remarks   106

6.6 Numerical Example   109

7. Exchange Rate Adjustment

7.1 The Free-Trade Exchange Rate   121

7.2 Methods to Estimate the Free-Trade Exchange Rate 127

8. Net Protection

8.1 Net Effective Protection   139

8.2 Exchange Rate Adjustment, Non-Tradables and
    Indirect Taxes   142

8.3 Average Net Protection   148

9.   The Structure of Protection in Mexico in 1980

9.1 Protection in Mexico   153

9.2 Nominal Protection   158

9.3 Effective Protection   164

10. Summary   179

     References   188

     Author Index   192

     Subject Index   194

vii

List of tables and diagrams

4.1   The Nominal Rate of Protection: no exchange rate
      adjustment   38
4.2   The Nominal Rate of Protection: with exchange rate
      adjustment   42
4.3   Allowed Ranges for the Nominal Rate of Protection   53
5.1   Input-Output Table at Basic Prices in the Protection
      Situation   70
5.2   Input-Output Table: at free-trade prices   75
5.3   Decomposition of Effective Protection   77
5.4   Input-Output Table: at producers' prices   82
5.5   Net Indirect Taxes   83
5.6   Input-Output Table: at basic prices   84
5.7   Input-Output Table: at free prices (original
      Balassa method)   86
5.8   Effective Protection   87
5.9   Decomposition of Effective Protection (original
      Balassa method)   88
6.1   Contracted Input-Output Table: at real prices   102
6.2   Input-Ouptut Table: values at free-trade prices
      (modified Balassa method)   110
6.3   Effective Protection by Sector (modified Balassa method)   111
6.4   Decomposition of Effective Protection (modified Balassa
      method)   111
6.5   Input-Output Table: values at free-trade prices
      (original Scott method)   112
6.6   Effective Protection by Sector (original Scott method)   113

6.7   Input-Output Table: values at free trade prices
       (modified Scott method)   114
6.8   Effective Protection by Sector (modified Scott method)   114
6.9   Effective Protection by Sector (original Corden method)   115
6.10   Contracted Input-Output Table: at protection prices
       (modified Corden method)   116
6.11   Contracted Input-Output Table: at free trade prices
       (modified Corden method)   117
6.12   Effective Protection by Sector (modified Corden method)   118
6.13   Decomposition of Effective Protection (modified Corden
       method)   119
6.14   Nominal and Effective Protection: comparative results   120
9.1   Economic Activity Classification   159
9.2   Sample Composition   161
9.3   Nominal Protective Rates by Sector in Mexico in 1980   162
9.4   Effective Protection in Mexico in 1980 (original
       Balassa method)   167
9.5   Effective Protection in Mexico in 1980: under various
       treatments of the non-tradables   170
9.6   Decomposition of Effective Protection: Mexico, 1980
       (modified Balassa method)   173
9.7   Net Effective Protection in Mexico in 1980 (original
       Balassa method)   177

Diagrams
4.1   Trade Character Changes: no exchange rate adjustment   36
4.2   Trade Character Changes under Exchange Rate Adjustment   40
4.3   Trade Character Changes under Exchange Rate Adjustment   41

Preface

This book is one of the byproducts of two research projects on the structure of protection in Mexico. The first of these started in the autumn of 1973 under the auspices of the National School of Economics of the National Autonomous University of Mexico (UNAM), in cooperation with the Centre for Development Planning of the Erasmus University, Rotterdam. As a member of the Centre I was involved in the preparation and coordination of this project and participated in all its stages; and Bruce Wallace acted as coordinator on behalf of UNAM. Subsequently we published the main results jointly, in Protection and Economic Development in Mexico (1980).

The second project was sponsored by the Mexican Ministry of Commerce and carried out in cooperation with the Mexican Institute of Foreign Trade (IMCE). Its aim was to update the protection estimates of former studies and set up an operational system to measure nominal and effective protection on a regular basis. I was invited in 1979 to take part in this on behalf of the Centre for Development Planning, and was involved from its start in July 1980.

The main ideas that are worked out in this book were conceived during the first study and are included in a concise form in Protection and Economic Development in Mexico. But taking part in the second project gave me the opportunity to develop and test them in an environment of policy making.

In acknowledgement I should like first to express my gratitude to Jan Tinbergen who helped me in 1968 to exchange theoretical physics, his own original discipline, for economics and guided my first steps in the new field.

Secondly my thanks are due to all those with whom I had the pleasure of cooperating during the practical work in Mexico. I am particularly grateful to Bruce Wallace, without whose active participation and continuous support it would have been impossible to publish the first study. He was also involved at a later stage in the second project and has revised the English of this material for publication.

I am also grateful to Fernando de Mateo, coordinator for the Ministry of Commerce; and to Carlos Piñera, Sergio Escamilla and all others in the team, who by carrying out much of the practical work and contributing several useful observations during its execution, have helped indirectly to bring the book about.

In addition I am glad to include Bela Balassa and the staff of the World Bank, with whom on a number of occasions I had the opportunity to discuss methodological and practical difficulties in the field.

Finally I should like to offer thanks to my colleagues at the Centre for Development Planning, particularly to Henk Bos who supervised this work and commented extensively on the manuscript; to Jacob Kol whose reading of the first four chapters led me to rewrite them to some extent; and to Solomon Cohen, Peter Cornelisse, Arie Kuyvenhoven and Loet Mennes for the support and interest they have shown in my work during its long gestation. I am also grateful to Karin Niepoth and Carla Verhoeff for typing the manuscript on a word processor and for teaching me to operate it myself when the numerous changes I wanted them to carry out had driven them to despair. And I owe Kees van Opijnen en Hennie de Keyzer much for preparing this trade edition.

Adriaan ten Kate

1 Introduction

1.1 Purpose and Scope of the Study

Economic policies restricting foreign trade are often applied in order to protect home industries from foreign competition. Import tariffs, for example, by raising the prices at which domestic purchasers have access to imported goods, allow domestic producers of similar goods to be competitive at higher prices than would otherwise have been possible. That is how domestic producers benefit indirectly from trade-restrictive policies and in this sense they are said to be protected. Therefore foreign-trade regimes are often referred to as systems of protection.

In so far as such policies provoke a distorted domestic price system, they may lead to misallocation of resources. Economic activities that would be inefficient when judged by a national-economic cost-benefit criterion based on accounting prices may become attractive under the distorted market prices, while other activities that are sound from a national-economic point of view may lose their profitability in an artificially adverse market. For that reason there is a strong interest in measuring the magnitude of the distortions and the protection derived from them, particularly for the purpose of sector and project evaluation.

There are two measures currently employed to quantify the protection granted to industries. These are nominal protection, which measures the impact of the system of protection upon the price of the industry's output; and effective protection, which takes explicit account of its influence on input costs and measures its impact upon the value-added that the industry generates with the production of its output.

In this study the definitions of these concepts and the assumptions on which they are based are examined critically. Particular attention is given to the way in which nominal protection is measured; systematic schemes are set up for the calculation of effective protection under the different assumptions of the valuation of non-tradable goods[1] and foreign exchange: and lastly a case study for Mexico is presented to illustrate the theory.

The purpose is first to try to strengthen the theoretical basis for the nominal and effective protection concepts; and secondly it is hoped, by suggesting a more systematic approach than can be found anywhere else, to bring the theory closer to practical application.

1.2   Outline of the Contents

In Chapter 2 the conceptual framework of the study is set up. Here some notes on estimating the effects of economic policy in general are followed by the particular case of a foreign-trade regime. A definition is given and the conditions that would obtain in the absence of such a regime, that is under free trade, are examined in detail. Then a definition of the concept, 'system of protection', is provided and finally the free-trade situation, is considered, that is, the situation that would materialise under conditions of free trade.

Nominal protection is the focal concept of Chapter 3, in which the nominal protective rate of a commodity is defined as the extent to which its existing price exceeds its hypothetical free-trade price, that is, the price it would assume under conditions of free trade. The assumptions underlying the estimated free-trade prices are explained; and in order to make nominal protection applicable to the output of a whole industry an aggregation device relates the nominal protective rate to baskets of heterogeneous goods.

None the less the measurement of nominal protection may present many difficulties. These form the subject of Chapter 4, where is argued that even if there are no quantitative restrictions in the foreign-trade regime, the classical tariff rate can only be a reasonable approximation

---

1. Non-tradable goods are those which cannot potentially be traded between countries. For example, buildings are non-tradeable. For a fuller description subsection 6.1.1.

of the nominal rate of protection for goods which are imported in reality. For exported goods and also for non-traded tradables the import tariff rate is of little help. If quantitative restrictions are applicable nominal protection can only be estimated by making price comparisons. The main difficulties encountered in this field are surveyed and the level of specification at which price comparisons should be carried out is argued. It is also explained how the foreign-trade regime together with the trade character of the goods considered can be used as a filter to reject false price comparisons from the product sample.

Chapter 5 deals with the concept of effective protection. The effective rate of protection of an activity is defined as the extent to which its value-added at existing prices exceeds that at free-trade prices; and a discussion follows of the assumptions on which the value added at free-trade prices is estimated. The main part of this text is devoted to an input-output approach, where it is shown that effective protection can be obtained by merely converting the valuation of an input-output table from existing to free-trade prices. To illustrate the procedure, the chapter closes with a numerical example.

The treatment of non-tradable goods and services in Chapter 6 surveys the concept of non-tradability and the options available for the valuation of the non-tradables at free-trade prices. The methods of Balassa and Scott are examined in different formulations and Corden's alternative treatment of the non-tradable inputs is discussed. It is demonstrated that any input-output table can be contracted in such a way that indirect[2] tradeable and primary inputs are grouped with the corresponding entries in the columns of the tradeables and final demand. In that way both rows and columns for the non-tradables disappear from the table but the totals of the remaining rows and columns remain unaffected. At the end there is a confrontation of the different possibilities and the numerical example of Chapter 5 is continued.

Chapter 7 deals with the free-trade valuation of foreign exchange. It is argued that the suppression of the system of protection is likely to provoke an imbalance in the balance of payments which requires an adjustment of the exchange rate. The usual way to estimate the magnitude

2. That is, through non-tradable inputs.

of the required adjustment is based on price elasticities of foreign-trade flows and is therefore called the elasticity approach. An alternative method, the purchasing-power approach, adjusts the exchange rate to an extent that purchasing-power parity is established between the free-trade and the existing situation. Both approaches are explained and worked out algebraically. To conclude there is a discussion of their pros and cons.

In Chapter 8 the exchange rate adjustments are used to convert ordinary rates of protection into net rates. It is shown that the assumptions of the free-trade prices of the non-tradables and the exchange rate adjustment are not completely independent. Also the assumption of domestic indirect taxation under free trade is examined in the light of exchange rate adjustment. Finally it is proved that with an adjustment according to the purchasing-power approach, average protection - both nominal and effective - can be made to disappear. Nominal protection then becomes a closed circuit of money transfers among the purchasers of domestic-final-demand goods, and effective protection becomes a circuit of transfers among the productive sectors and the government.

Chapter 9 presents a case study for Mexico. Following an outline of protection policies since the Second World War, especially during the late seventies, the study of the structure of protection in the Mexican economy in 1980 is reported and nominal and effective protection estimates are presented on an aggregation of 24 sectors, of which 5 sectors produce exclusively non-tradables. The results are used to illustrate the main topics of the previous chapters.

A note on currency. Where prices are tabled or quoted in the text the unit is the Mexican peso; a billion is a thousand million; and a dollar is a US dollar.

1.3   Contribution of the Study

The concepts of nominal and effective protection are not new. On the contrary, nominal protection for tariffs has been talked about ever since tariffs have been applied, and the first formal statement of the effective protective rate was made by Meade as early as 1955.[3] Similarly

3. See Meade (1955), vol. II, p. 157.

the treatment of the non-tradables and the free-trade valuation of foreign exchange have been widely discussed since 1965.[4] It may be useful therefore to indicate what, to the author's knowledge, the present study adds to the existing literature.

First it is designed to bring the theory closer to practice (See 1.1). To give an example: where the theory defines nominal protection in terms of prices, it is suggested what sort of prices to take - producer or consumer, including or excluding indirect taxes, and so on - and for what reasons. Special attention is paid to problems of valuation and registration in input-output tables; while the theory the concept of effective protection is defined in terms of input-output coefficients without further clarification.

There are also a number of contributions in the theoretical sphere. The expression 'free-trade conditions' is well known to students of protection and it would be difficult to find a better definition; but here the interpretation acquires a more specific meaning. The fact that several other interpretations would have been possible may demonstrate the need for clarification on this point.

Many of the arguments in Chapter 4 on the measurement of nominal protection are new also. The relation between nominal protection and the trade regime worked out in the first section, together with the filter to reject false price comparisons, cannot be found elsewhere. Moreover the view adopted regarding the use of unit values for the purpose of price comparison is more tolerant than is customary in this field.

The input-output approach to effective protection presented in Chapter 5 where the effective rates are obtained from a revaluation of the input-output table at free-trade prices is not new in this work; but it is due to the same author. A more concise account of this approach is inlcuded in the theoretical appendix to Protection and Economic Development in Mexico.[5]

The discussion of average protection, the treatment of the non-tradables, the exchange rate adjustment, and net protection (Chapters 5 to 8), is closely related with the special input-output approach of

4. These subjects are extensively dealt with in Corden (1971) and Balassa et al. (1971).
5. See Ten Kate et al. (1980).

Chapter 5. Most of its elements are presented in the theoretical appendix mentioned above, but here they are worked out in more detail. The contraction of the input-output table with the modified Corden method, proposed in Chapter 6, is new.

Finally, the material for the case study is drawn from the unpublished papers of the Mexican Ministry of Commerce project, in which the author collaborated. Its methodology is roughly the same one that is developed in this book. Therefore the results of the Mexican study and the case study presented in Chapter 9 may be considered a proper test of its workability.

2 Conceptual framework

2.1 Assessing the Effects of Economic Policy

To quantify the effects of a set of economic-policy measures it is necessary to compare two situations: the with-policy situation with such measures in force; and the without-policy situation in which the package is not operative. If the set of policy measures is in the proposal stage the without-policy situation may be identified with the existing situation but the with-policy situation must be estimated. If on the other hand the policy package has been operative long enough to be effective the with-policy situation can be observed realistically but the without-policy situation must be estimated.

Either way, one of the situations will be hypothetical, so it is hardly feasible to expect to define the effects of the measures with absolute certainty: on the contrary it all depends on how the hypothetical situation is estimated and obviously such estimation may be controversial. If, for example, a new tax system was introduced a few years ago it would be tempting to ascribe any changes in tax revenues to the tax reform and in so doing implicitly interpret the present situation as with-policy, while identifying the without-policy situation with what existed before the tax reform. As far as the with-policy situation is concerned no objections can be made provided the time-lag is not too short. The identification of the without-policy situation with the past however is questionable. No doubt some changes would have occurred had the old tax system remained in force. Thus the reform can only be held responsible for part of the total changes, and to find that part it is unavoidable to estimate the situation that would have developed under the old tax regime, but with all other elements of change taken into account. The without-policy situation ob-tained in this way may be substantially different from the pre-reform realities. Moreover its approximation is subject to all kinds of uncertainties inherent in projecting and estimating economic variables.

With that in mind it seems virtually impossible to assess the impact of any policy package indisputably. Lack of agreement on such matters is reflected in everlasting debate on economic policy all over the world. Is a sudden decrease of unemployment the result of a special

employment programme adopted by the government? Would it have occurred
anyway? Is a bad growth performance of an economy due to bad government
administration or despite a good one? Those are the sort of questions
that are posed and as long as political interests are strong their
answers are not likely to be unique.

   None the less the ambiguities should not be exaggerated. For some
areas of economic policy they are stronger than for others and for some
economic variables the impact of the policy measures can be assessed
more reliably than for others. As mentioned in the introduction, this
work deals with one specific area of economic policy, namely the
foreign-trade regime, and the effects studied are those which impinge on
the prices of tradable goods and on the value-added generated by
producing them. Even though it is necessary to make a number of
simplifying assumptions about prices in the without-policy situation,
the impact of a foreign-trade regime upon prices and value-added per
unit of production can be quantified more reliably than can many other
economic-policy instruments and their impact upon other economic
variables.

   To simplify the terminology, it is assumed that the foreign-trade
regimes examined exist in reality, that is, the with-policy situation is
the existing situation, now to be called the protection situation, and
the without-policy situation is the hypothetical situation obtained in
the absence of a foreign-trade regime, to be called the free-trade
situation. Where the trade-regulating measures are in the proposal stage
the required terminological changes are all straightforward.

2.2   Foreign-Trade Regimes

   A foreign-trade regime means the set of all those instruments of
economic policy that national governments apply to regulate the foreign
trade of the country. The most commonly used in any foreign-trade regime
are import tariffs, export taxes and subsidies and import and export
licens-ing. Whether the instruments intentionally or unintentionally
protect or fail to protect home industries, whether they are trade-
restrictive or stimulating, is not relevant. To be in the regime, the
instruments must explicitly apply to foreign-trade transactions. For
example, tax rebates on exportation form part of the regime but soft
loans to agriculture do not, even though the latter may be granted with

the aim of increasing exports or substituting imports.

The instruments of a foreign-trade regime can be roughly classified in two groups. The first consists of all those measures which have a direct influence on the domestic prices that exporters receive or importers have to pay once they engage in foreign-trade transactions. These are price measures and comprise all kinds of tariffs, sur-charges and subsidies applicable to imports or exports, and of course multiple-exchange-rate regulations, if they are resorted to. Generally policies having a direct incidence on the currency exchange rate also belong to this group. All measures affecting entitlement to engage in foreign-trade transactions fall into the second category, that of quantitative restrictions, which comprises import and export licensing, quota regulations and quality controls, among others.

2.3 Free Trade

To make the trade of a country free it is not enough that the foreign-trade regime in the sense of section 2.2 is abolished. For instance, other countries may apply trade-regulating meas-ures which will affect the first-named country as well, so that its trade would not be completely free. Secondly, not all trade is foreign trade. Thus to make all trade free it would be necessary to abolish policies affecting internal trade also.

There is no concern here about the trade regimes of other countries. In fact for the one country considered trade is already said to be free whenever no such trade-regulating measures are applicable, irrespective of whether its trade partners or any other countries apply trade regulations. This implies that the effect its foreign-trade regime may have upon other countries' regimes is not considered. On the contrary it is assumed that with the elimination of its own foreign-trade regime the regimes of the other countries remain unchanged.

Clearly that is an oversimplification. It may well be that a country would use the elimination of its foreign-trade regime to obtain con-cessions in the regimes of trade- partner countries; for example, in the form of lower import tariffs on its exports. However owing to the unpredictable nature of such mutual concessions (or retaliations), there is no other way than assuming ceteris-paribus conditions in the trade regimes of other countries.

The connection of the foreign-trade regime with policies affecting trade within the country is usually stronger. In particular policies to control domestic prices and also the indirect-tax system generally are closely related to policies regulating foreign trade. Indeed it is hardly conceivable that the foreign-trade regime could be eliminated without a number of concurrent adjustments in these related areas.

To give an example, let us say that domestic price control policies keep the price of a certain product lower in the domestic market than in the export market. If there were no export limitations in the form of taxes or licensing, domestic supply would be exported and the domestic market would dry up. Thus the export limitation which forms part of the foreign-trade regime cannot be eliminated without giving up the price control at the same time.

The easiest way to avoid this sort of complication is always to consider the foreign and internal-trade regimes together in one package. Trade would then be free when the whole policy package was abolished. In this study however it is preferred to keep as closely as possible to the foreign-trade regime as such, including with it only those elements of internal-trade policies that cannot feasibly be retained if the foreign-trade regime is eliminated. What this implies in terms of the indirect-tax system and other internal-trade policies is explained in section 2.5.

2.4   Systems of Protection

The expression, system of protection, stands for an extension of the foreign-trade regime in the sense of section 2.3. It is defined as the set of policy measures contained in the foreign-trade regime, complemented by all those measures in related fields which cannot feasibly be kept in force when eliminating the foreign-trade regime. A description of complementary measures is given below,but here a few observations would be in order.

It should be recognised, following this defini-tion, that a system of protection includes certain elements which do not or are not meant to protect home industries. For example, import regulations for final-consumption goods that do not compete with domestic supply neither protect nor discriminate against any home industry. On the other hand the system of protection thus defined does not cover a number of widely applied policy instruments which definitely protect home industries and are meant to do so. Wage cost subsidies, for example, provide outright protection to the receiving industry but as they are not usually related to the foreign-trade regime, they do not form part of the system of protection according to the definition. Similar observations can be made about other sorts of subsidies not related to foreign trade, such as soft loans, domestic-tax exemptions and so on.

The indirect-tax system in particular may be full of discriminatory elements. For that reason it is often included in the system of protection.[1] In the above definition this is not so be-cause the domestic part of the indirect-tax system can be maintained perfectly when the foreign-trade regime is abolished. This definition is therefore preferred, to avoid mixing up the effects of measures applied to foreign trade with those of domestic indirect taxes.

The exclusion of domestic indirect taxation from the system of protection makes the formulation of effective protection somewhat more complicated than it would otherwise have been. But it sheds some light on a number of subtleties which usually remain under the surface. For the inclusion of the whole indirect-tax system in the system of protection, the modifications are straightforward and can be performed by the reader. The same holds true for the inclusion of subsidies and other sorts of protective measures not included in the definition.

1. In the intercountry study on the structure of protection in developing countries directed by Balassa, the indirect-tax system of the country is supposed to form part of the system of protection. That is to say, it is assumed that in the free-trade situation the indirect-tax system is also abolished. Although this is not stated explicitly, it can be derived from the way in which indirect taxes are treated in the definition of the effec-tive rate. See Balassa et al. (1971), App. A, p. 320. A similar interpretation is adopted by Corden. See Corden(1971), ch. 3, pp. 40-45.

2.5   Indirect Taxes under Free Trade

The indirect-tax measures, which are supposed to be abolished with
the foreign-trade regime, are here indicated. This is done partly by
showing which indirect taxes are assumed to remain in force under free
trade and in what form.

There can be little doubt about indirect taxes such as import
tariffs, export taxes and so on, as they form part of the foreign-trade
regime itself and they are automatically eliminated with the regime.
The same holds true for special tax exemptions granted for the purpose
of export promotion. Such exemptions may refer to all sorts of taxes:
corporate-income tax, indirect taxes on inputs,and so on. As they also
form part of the foreign-trade regime, they are not supposed to be
granted under free trade.

However there is one important exception. If indirect commodity
taxes to be paid on domestic products are paid back, or are not charged
on exportation, this is supposed to remain the same under free trade. In
fact that is the normal situation, otherwise domestic suppliers to
international markets would be placed in an unfavourable position vis-à
vis foreign competitors. Thus if in reality such indirect commodity
taxes are not paid back on exportation, it is is considered as an
element of negative protection.

The paying back of indirect commodity taxes on exportation is an
example of the application of the so-called destination principle.
According to this, indirect taxes only become payable in the act of
purchasing by the consumer.[2] Opposite to the destination principle, the
origin principle demands payment of indirect taxes in the act of selling
by the producer.

Thus it is assumed that indirect commodity taxes under free trade
operate according to the destination principle. The implications for
exported products are spelt out above. On the import side it implies
that imported products are subject to the same indirect taxation as
their domestically produced equivalents. If in reality indirect taxes
payable on domestic production are not charged on equivalent imports, it
implies that a part of the import tariff is considered to substitute the
indirect tax and only the remaining part belongs to the system of

2. ibid., ch. 2, p. 17.

protection. Thus if in practice indirect commodity taxes do not operate according to the destination principle the elimination of the foreign-trade taxes should go hand in hand with the appropriate border tax adjustments.

To give an example, let us say that a product is subject to a domestic sales tax of 15 per cent ad valorem which is not paid back if the product is exported. In such a case it is convenient to consider the tax paid on the exported product not as a domestic indirect tax but as an export tax, which for that reason would be abolished with the elimination of the system of protection.

It seems reasonable to treat indirect taxation on the exploitation of depletable natural resources, and also the other non-commodity taxes, in a different way. If not, the principle adopted could lead to a situation where, for example, an international oil company, which in practice pays an indirect tax on every barrel of crude oil produced, would not pay any compensation to the country under free trade. The existing indirect tax would thus be interpreted as an element of negative protection. Such indirect taxes are here interpreted as the price the oil company pays to the country, the latter being the legal owner of the depletable resources, and thus it is assumed that these taxes remain in force under free trade. Generally it is assumed that in the free trade situation indirect taxes on exploitation of depletable natural resources and other non-commodity taxes operate according to the origin principle. This implies that no such taxes are paid back on exportation and that imports of such goods are not subject to that sort of domestic taxation. They are supposed to be taxed in the country where they came from.

Finally something should be said about the basis of indirect taxation. Roughly there are two possibilities. Indirect taxation may be either on an ad-valorem basis, that is, taxes are expressed as a percentage of value; or on a specific basis, that is they are expressed as a certain amount of money per unit of goods transacted.

If it is assumed that the indirect taxes which remain in force under free trade should do so on an ad-valorem basis, the amount of taxes payable per physical unit would vary with the elimination of the system of protection, as the price the goods would assume under free trade will usually be different from the price assumed in reality. In

this way, there would still be a connection between the system of
protection and the domestic part of the indirect-tax system.

    To avoid this connection it is assumed that the relevant indirect
taxes remain in force on a specific basis. In that case the amount of
taxes payable per physical unit remains the same, irrespective of the
price change the goods might undergo as a result of the elimination of
the system of protection. If in practice these taxes are formulated on
ad-valorem terms this assumption implies either a rephrasing in specific
terms or an adjustment of the ad-valorem rate to the free-trade
conditions.

    The assumptions adopted in this section are arbitrary to a certain
degree. Depending on the purpose of study it may be preferable to take a
different point of view. For instance the complete indirect-tax system
might be incorporated in the system of protection, as in other studies,
or in another part of the system. It would be laborious to cover all
possibilities but requisite adjustments are straightforward and can be
performed by the reader. This study is confined to the above described
case. Only in section 8.2. can a concise description be given of the
changes to be carried out in the effective-protection calculations where
the indirect-tax system is assumed to remain in force on an ad-valorem
basis.

2.6   Price Control under Free Trade

    The title, price control under free trade, seems to be a
'contradictio in terminis' and indeed the example given in section 2.3
shows clearly how policies to control domestic prices may be
incompatible with the conditions prevailing under free trade. However in
the special meaning given here to the concept of free trade there may
still be room for some price control policies in the free-trade
situation. It is the aim of this section to explore the possibility.

    Throughout the following chapters it is assumed that the free-
trade prices of tradable goods are dictated by international
quotations.[3] If the goods are imported under free trade the free-trade
price is supposed to be equal to the international price, with a
correction ajustment upwards to the margins necessary to bring the goods

---

3. See subsection 3.3.3.

from the international market to the country; or if the goods are
exported, the adjustment is downwards. In both cases however the price
of the goods is fixed and any policy measures aiming at another price
would be at odds with the free-trade conditions.

If a tradable product is non-traded under free trade, its free-
trade price is not completely fixed by its international price, as it is
for the traded goods. In fact there is a certain margin available –
between its potential f.o.b. export price and c.i.f. import price – for
the free-trade price to move and price control policies become feasible
within this margin. The less the tradability of the goods, the larger
the margin, and for completely non-tradable goods price control policies
are no longer incompatible with the absence of foreign-trade
regulations.

In order not to complicate matters unnecessarily it is assumed
here that for all goods classified as tradable, price control policies
are eliminated together with the system of protection, while for the
non-tradables they are not. This would imply that price control policies
for the non-tradables should persist under free trade. However as the
prices the non-tradables would assume under free trade are usually fixed
by assumption[4], price control policies for the non-tradeables are
implicitly assumed to be adjusted so as to fit the assumption adopted.

2.7   Free-Trade Conditions

Summarising the discussion of the previous sections, the trade of
a country is said to be free if the following conditions are met:

i. All commodities can enter the country freely without being charged
   tariffs or otherwise and without being subsidised in any form.
   Within the country, the commodities are charged with the same
   indirect commodity tax as their domestically produced equivalents,
   but non-commodity taxes, particularly those on the exploitation of
   depletable natural resources, are not due on the importation of
   such commodities.

---

4. A discussion of alternative assumptions for the free-trade prices of
   the non-tradables is given in Chapter 6.

   ii. All commodities can leave the country freely without being charged
      export taxes or otherwise and without being subsidised in any form
      whatsoever. Domestic indirect taxes on commodities are not due on
      their exportation. Non-commodity taxes however must be paid anyway.
  iii. Foreign exchange is treated as if it were a tradable commodity.
      This implies the absence of direct exchange controls and of
      multiple-exchange rate regulations. Domestic currency is freely
      convertible and the exchange rate is the result of market forces.
   iv. There is no government intervention in the price formation of
      tradable commodities.

If the point of departure is an existing protection situation, it is
furthermore assumed that all other elements of economic policy within
the country and policies of other countries are the same as in the
protection situation.

2.8   Free-Trade Situation

The free-trade situation is that which would be obtained under
free-trade conditions. It is not however the situation produced
immediately after an abrupt elimination of the system of protection. It
is rather the situation that would have developed, had the system of
protection been abolished a long time ago. It is implicitly assumed that
the way in which this was done and how long ago it took place are not
relevant. In other words it is assumed that the free-trade situation is
uniquely defined.

Since the free-trade situation is of a hypothetical nature it
would be a very difficult, if not an impossible task, to simulate its
characteristics extensively. To find free-trade values for the main
variables of national accounts - production and consumption levels,
imports, exports, prices, input-output relations, value added - it would
be necessary to specify a general- equilibrium model in all those
variables, estimate its parameters and obtain its solution. It is
needless to mention the difficulties inherent in model specification,
parameter estimation and electronic computation.

Fortunately the knowledge of the free-trade situation required for
the estimation of nominal and effective protection is much more limited.
To assess nominal protection it is necessary to know the free-trade

prices of the tradable goods and for effective protection free-trade prices for all goods and services are required. The free-trade prices for the tradables can be approximated by means of international prices and those for the non-tradables are usually defined by certain assumptions which are not too unreasonable. Thus for the measurement of nominal and effective protection no such complicated matters as general-equilibrium models are necessary.

Roughly it may be said that nominal and effective protection only require the knowledge of free-trade prices, not of free-trade quantities. That does not imply that it would not be interesting to know free-trade quantities as well. On the contrary, only then it would be possible to assess the impact of the system of protection upon a number of extremely relevant economic variables such as production, consumption, employment and so on . However that is beyond the scope of the nominal and effective-protection concepts. Nominal and effective protection should be conceived as short-cuts. They measure the strength of the pulls and pushes exercised by the protective system upon the sectors of the economy, but they do not measure the response of those sectors, however interesting the latter might be.

No attempt is made here to estimate the values which quantity variables would assume in the free-trade situation. Even when valuations are at free-trade prices, quantities are usually taken from the protection situation. In other words, apart from a few exceptions, this study is not concerned with the free-trade situation as such, but rather with a valuation of the protection situation at free-trade prices.

3 Nominal protection

3.1 Background

3.1.1 The Nominal Tariff Rate

The most elementary manner to quantify the strength of the protection derived from an import tariff is to measure it by the <u>nominal tariff rate</u> expressed on an ad-valorem basis, that is the amount of tariffs payable expressed as a percentage of import value. The idea is that competition between domestic production and supply from abroad equalises prices so that the impact of the tariff system upon the prices of goods produced in the country is equal to that upon the prices of equivalent goods on the import bill. Hence the nominal tariff rate expresses the protection granted to domestic producers in terms of the relative increase in the prices of their output. The early literature on the subject focuses on the case where protection is practically synonymous with tariff protection and it is the nominal rate of tariff protection which receives most attention.[1]

An important aspect of the nominal tariff rate is that its measurement is comparatively easy. In the case of uniform and purely ad-valorem tariffs it can be read straight from the tariff lists. Complications may arise when the country participates in international-integration schemes or other forms of trade agreements, or when specific importers are eligible for tariff exemption or rebates, but in all cases reasonable estimates of nominal tariff protection can be obtained by setting total tariff revenues on the considered item against the value of imports.

There is however one important reason to believe that the concept of nominal tariff protection, even when the foreign-trade regime consists exclusively of tariffs, is of limited use. The argument is that for most countries a good deal of domestic production does not really enter into competition with imports. When competition between domestic products and similar imported products is less than perfect or, what is even more serious, when no product equivalent to the domestically produced goods can be found on the import bill of the country, the

---

1. See Soligo and Stern (1965); Balassa (1965); and Corden (1966), among others.

nominal tariff rate - if it is possible to find such a rate - may considerably overestimate the tariff's impact on the domestic price. In Chapter 4, these different cases are spelt out.

Another important limitation to the use of the nominal tariff rate as a measure for the protective effects of a foreign-trade regime is that, on many occasions, tariffs are complemented with licensing and other quantitative restrictions. If that is so, it is possible that the protective effect which derives from such quantitative restrictions grossly exceeds protection resulting from the tariff part of the regime. Consequently in such cases the nominal tariff rate can never be a good proxy for the regime's impact upon domestic-price levels.

3.1.2 The Implicit Nominal Rate

Developing countries particularly, attempting to industrialise through policies of import substitution, often rely heavily on quantitative trade restrictions. Therefore it is not surprising that, once the attention of empirical protection studies had shifted from the developed to the developing economies, it was realised that the conventional way of measuring nominal protection through tariffs was inadequate.[2] The alternative is to measure the regime's direct impact on domestic-price levels. That is by comparing existing domestic prices with international quotations, the latter being used as proxies for the prices which would prevail in the domestic market under conditions of free trade.

The nominal protective rate resulting from such price comparisons is usually called the implicit nominal rate, in contrast to the nominal tariff rate that results from the conventional form of measurement. Rather than merely assuming that the price increase of the imported goods caused by the tariff is directly translated into a corresponding price increase of the domestically produced equivalent, the implicit nominal rate checks whether the domestic price is indeed so much higher than the international price. As such, the implicit rate measures the regime's impact upon domestic price levels more directly than the tariff rate and should therefore be preferred even when the foreign-trade regime cnsists solely of tariffs.

2. Lewis and Guisinger (1968), in their study of protection in Pakistan, state this problem explicitly.

It must be realised however that it is more complicated to measure nominal protection through price comparison. The price of the same goods may vary from one location to another, from one day to another, from one purchaser to another, and it will not always be so easy to know which price to take. Moreover while setting the domestic price of goods produced in the country against international quotations it must be clear that all characteristics of the domestic goods are indeed identical to their traded counterpart, so as not to attribute to the trade regime price differences that are due to other factors, such as quality differences and so on.

With this in mind it seems virtually impossible to measure implicit nominal protection for all tradable goods produced in an economy and it must be admitted that indeed it is impossible. Nevertheless by establishing price comparisons on a sampling basis, including as many products as possible but giving more emphasis to those products which represent an important share of domestic production, a much better idea is obtained of the potential competitive position of a country in international trade than can be learned from tariff rates.

3.2   The Nominal Rate of Protection of a Product

3.2.1 Definition

Here the nominal protective rate of a product is defined as the extent to which the existing protection price of that product exceeds the price which would have prevailed in the domestic market under conditions of free trade. Denoting the existing protection price by p and the free-trade price in the domestic market by p^{ft}, the nominal protective rate w can be expressed as:

$$(3.1) \qquad w = \frac{p - p^{ft}}{p^{ft}}$$

This definition coincides with the interpretation of the rate of protection adopted by Corden, in The Theory of Protection,[3] where a discussion can be found of a number of alternative interpretations of the concept. The more practical interpretation of the nominal protective

3. See Corden (1971), ch 2, pp. 21- 7.

rate as the proportional divergence between the domestic and the foreign price[4] has the disadvantage that it does not make clear what sort of corrections should be applied to the foreign price in order to bring it in line with the domestic price. Moreover the assumptions establishing the link with the foreign-trade regime remain implicit.[5] For these reasons to the former interpretation is preferred.

In the definition adopted there is one concept in need of further clarification. It is that of price.

3.2.2 The Price of the Product

In order to be assigned a nominal rate of protection a product must be priceable, that is, it must be so specific that it can have a well-defined price. Raw cotton, for example, is too general. Perhaps raw cotton, middling 1 inch, is specific enough. But even for completely specified products prices may vary from one transaction to another for different reasons. Moreover the price usually increases on its way from the producer to the consumer. Indirect taxation may cause producers' prices to be higher than basic prices, whereas wholesale and retail prices may be higher still as a result of trade and transport margins.

Therefore, because it is the protection given to the group of domestic producers that is to be quantified, it is in principle the producers' price which is the relevant one. However, given the assumptions for the indirect-tax system under free trade, these producers' prices should be taken net of indirect commodity taxes to put them on the same footing as free-trade prices. In other words it is the basic prices[6] that should be taken.

If protection is measured over a period, as is usually done, the best method to follow is to take the average basic price over all units produced during that period. The free-trade price on the other hand should be conceived as the average maximum basic price at which domestic producers could sell their products and still be competitive with

4. See for example Balassa et al. (1971), ch.1, p. 4.
5. These assumptions are discussed in section 3.3.
6. The term 'basic price' of a commodity stands for its price net of trade and transport margins and net of indirect commodity taxes. No deductions are made to correct for non-commodity taxes, nor for indirect commodity taxes on inputs; that is, the basic price corresponds with the approximate basic value concept in the sense of national accounts. See United Nations (1968), annex to ch. 4.

foreign suppliers under con-ditions of free trade.

To estimate the levels at which prices would settle under free-trade conditions, several assumptions must be made. These are discussed section 3.3 where the implications of working with basic prices are spelt out in more detail.

3.3   Assumptions Underlying the Estimation of Free-Trade Prices

3.3.1 Perfect Competition

First, it is assumed that the domestic free-trade price p^{ft} of a commodity is equal to its free-trade world market price multiplied by the free-trade exchange rate plus a correction accounting for trade and transport margins. This can be expressed in the following way:

$$(3.2) \qquad p^{ft} = r^{ft} \pi^{ft} (1 + b^{ft})$$

where r^{ft} is the free-trade exchange rate in domestic currency per unit of foreign currency,

π^{ft} the free-trade world market price in foreign currency units

b^{ft} the corrective term expressed as a fraction of the world market price.

If under free trade the product competes with imports, the corrective term accounts for trade and transport margins to be paid to bring the product from the world market to the domestic market and is positive. If the product is exported the correction is negative and stands for the margins necessary to get it from the domestic to the world market. In subsections 3.3.4 and 3.3.5 the corrective term is explained in more detail.

Formula (3.2) would be correct if competition between world and domestic markets was perfect under free-trade conditions. Therefore this assumption is referred to as the perfect-competition assumption.

3.3.2 The Small Country

A second step towards the estimation of the domestic free-trade price is to assume that the free-trade world market price is equal to the actual world market price:

(3.3) $\pi^{ft} = \pi$

This will be the case if world market supply and demand conditions are
such that the country cannot exercise any influence on the world market
price by varying its own supply or demand. This is the so-called small-
country assumption.[7]

3.3.3 The Exchange Rate

Thirdly an assumption must be made regarding the exchange rate
which would prevail in the free-trade situation. Because most foreign-
trade regimes are more restrictive on the import than on the export
side, their elimination would lead to a considerably higher import bill
which would not be covered by a corresponding increase in export
revenues. For that reason it would not usually be possible to maintain
the original exchange rate under the new conditions. None the less the
normal assumption is that the existing protection exchange rate also
holds in the free-trade situation:

(3.4a) $r^{ft} = r$

Alternatively, if it is assumed that the exchange rate is adjusted with
the elimination of the foreign-trade regime, that is:

(3.4b) $r^{ft} = r (1 + \phi)$

where ϕ stands for the magnitude of the adjustment in relative terms;
then the resulting nominal rates of protection are called net nominal
rates as against ordinary nominal rates in the absence of such an
adjustment. The extent to which the exchange rate should be adjusted is
taken up in Chapter 7.

3.3.4 Trade and Transport Margins

Finally some assumptions must be made in respect of the corrective
term b^{ft}. First of all it should be understood that this term is

7. See Corden (1971), ch. 2, p. 5.

intended to translate the international price π^{ft} (through the exchange rate r^{ft}) into the maximum basic price at which domestic producers can sell the product and still be competitive with international supply. To that end two sorts of trade and transport margins must be accounted for:

i. margins necessary to bring the product from the domestic producer to the consumer, either in the country itself or abroad;
ii. margins necessary to bring the product from the international market, where price π^{ft} holds, to the consumer.

The corrective term b^{ft} must be equal to the difference between the latter and the former margins, both expressed as a percentage of the international price π^{ft}.

If the product is imported - that is the consumer is domestic - normally the latter margins are higher than the former and their difference is usually supposed to be equal to the margins necessary to bring the product from the international market to the country's custom-houses. This is equivalent to assuming that, under free trade, domestic producers cannot set their prices higher than c.i.f. import prices if they want to remain competitive with supply from abroad. Although it may be argued against this that domestic producers' plants can be located closer to the consumer markets than the points through which imports enter the country, it is not very likely that such differences would lead to important distortions. Therefore it is assumed in the following that, whenever the good is imported in the free-trade situation, the corrective term ($b^{ft} = b^{ft}_{imp}$) raises the international price π^{ft} of the product to its c.i.f. import price p^{ft}_{imp}:

$$(3.5) \qquad p^{ft}_{imp} = r^{ft} \pi^{ft}_{imp} = r^{ft} \pi^{ft} (1 + b^{ft}_{imp})$$

where π^{ft}_{imp} is the foreign currency import price.

If on the other hand the product is exported under free-trade conditions, the margins necessary to bring the product from the domestic producer to the consumer abroad would probably be higher than if it came direct from the international market. Leading the exported product through the international market, the corrective term ($b^{ft} = b^{ft}_{exp}$) must

be chosen, equal to minus the margins necessary to bring the product
from the domestic producer to the international market, and the basic
price at which the product is exportable can be written as:

$$(3.6) \quad p_{exp}^{ft} = r^{ft} \pi_{exp}^{ft} = r^{ft} \pi^{ft} (1 - b_{exp}^{ft})$$

where π_{exp}^{ft} is the foreign-currency export price. It is important to note
that the export price π_{exp}^{ft} is not the foreign-currency f.o.b. export
price. It is slightly lower because the margins necessary to bring the
product from the domestic producer f.o.b. in the port of exportation may
not be included.

It would be a difficult task to estimate accurately the magnitude
of trade and transport margins under free-trade conditions. Fortunately,
that is only of minor importance since as a rule these margins are small
in comparison with the product's price which in its turn can only be
assessed to a limited degree of accuracy. With that in mind, it is
readily assumed that these margins are not affected by the elimination
of the trade regime and that all superscripts ,'ft' on the corrective
terms b may be suppressed.

3.3.5 The Trade Character

A more problematic issue in this context is the product's trade
character under free trade, that is, whether it would be exported,
imported or non-traded.[8] This is of more importance because it defines
whether the corrective term should be positive or negative. As a
consequence incorrect estimations of the trade character lead to much
greater distortions than imprecise estimations of the magnitude of the
margins.

To decide whether goods would be imported, exported or non-traded,
the following prices are considered:

8. The possibility that goods would be imported and exported at the same
   time is not considered here. In the light of recent discussions on
   intra-industry and two-way trade this may seem an important omission.
   But it is understood that the condition of priceability implies a
   much higher level of product specification than is customary in the
   theory of intra-industry trade. See Kol et al. (1983).

    i. the existing protection price p,

   ii. the <u>potential import price</u> p_{imp}^{ft}. This price is given by formula (3.5). It is called the potential import price, because it is possible that the product is not imported in reality,

  iii. the <u>potential export price</u> p_{exp}^{ft} , as defined by formula (3.6).

Then it is assumed that the trade character of the goods in the free-trade situation depends on the position of the existing protection price with regard to the potential import and export prices. If the existing protection price is higher than the potential import price, the product is supposed to be imported. If it is lower than the potential export price the assumption is that the product is exported, and if it is between the potential import and export prices, it is assumed non-traded.

3.3.6 The Free-Trade Price

From the foregoing assumptions it follows that, should the product be imported in the free-trade situation, its free-trade price would be equal to its potential import price. If on the other hand the product was exported its free-trade price would be equal to its potential export price. Unfortunately the previous exposition does not provide a clear-cut device for the estimation of free-trade prices for tradable goods that happen to be non-traded under free trade.

In principle something could be said about the price at which domestic supply and demand would balance with the aid of a general-equilibrium model.[9] But the fact is that only a small minority of the tradable goods would be classified as non-traded under free trade, so it seems preferable to avoid that kind of complication and make some additional assumptions instead.

As systems of protection are usually more trade restrictive than trade stimulative, most products that would not be traded under free trade are not traded in the protection situation either. For these

---

9. See also the discussion of the general-equilibrium approach in subsection 6.1.3.

products the easiest way to proceed is to assume that their free-trade
price is equal to the existing protection price and to choose the
corrective term accordingly.[10] In that case the corrective term has
little to do with trade and transport margins but, rather, serves to
close the gap between the domestic and the international price of the
goods concerned. As a consequence of this assumption the nominal
protective rate of the product will be zero.

3.4 Ordinary versus Net Nominal Protective Rates

3.4.1 Standard Conversion Rule

The domestic free-trade prices obtained with the assumptions set
out in section 3.3. can be used to calculate the nominal rates of
protection according to their definition (3.1). If the unadjusted free-
trade exchange rate (3.4a) is chosen, the ordinary nominal protective
rates are obtained. If an adjusted free-trade exchange rate according to
(3.4b) is used, the resulting rates are called net nominal protective
rates. By first substituting the unadjusted (3.4a) and then the adjusted
exchange rate (3.4b) through the free-trade prices (3.2) into the
definition of the nominal protective rate (3.1), it is readily verified
that, provided the corrective term is not affected by the exchange rate
adjustment, the following relation holds between the ordinary rate w and
the net rate $\bar{w}$:

$$(3.7) \qquad (1 + w) = (1 + \phi)(1 + \bar{w})$$

where ϕ stands for the magnitude of the adjustment.

With the aid of this relation it is possible to express net rates
in terms of ordinary rates in the following way:

$$(3.8) \qquad \bar{w} = \frac{1 + w}{1 + \phi} - 1$$

With positive ϕ - that is, the adjustment implies a devaluation of the
country's currency - all net rates result systematically lower than the

10. By doing so, these goods are treated in the same way as the non-
    tradables in the original Balassa method. See subsection 6.2.1.

corresponding ordinary rates, as is to be expected.

Formula (3.8) is the standard rule to convert ordinary nominal rates of protection into net rates. It is used in all studies of protection whenever exchange rate adjustments are applied,[11] and is also used here. But it is only valid if the corrective term b is not affected by the exchange rate adjustment. In the subsection 3.4.2 some attention is given to the opposite case.

3.4.2 Non-Standard Conversion

To begin with it is necessary to distinguish between two free-trade situations: the one in which the exchange rate is not adjusted, to be called the unadjusted free-trade situation; and the adjusted free-trade situation in which the exchange rate is different from that of the protection situation. Denoting the corrective term for the unadjusted situation by b and for the adjusted situation by $\bar{b}$, it can be shown that the standard relation (3.7) can be generalised into:

$$(3.9) \qquad (1 + w) = \frac{1 + \bar{b}}{1 + b} (1 + \phi)(1 + \bar{w})$$

and the standard conversion rule (3.8) into:

$$(3.10) \qquad \bar{w} = \frac{(1 + b)(1 + w)}{(1 + \bar{b})(1 + \phi)} - 1$$

Where the adjusted and unadjusted corrective terms are equal, the generalised rule coincides with the standard rule.

Whether or not the correction for trade and transport margins is affected by the exchange rate adjustment depends mainly on the trade character of the product in these two situations. If the product is imported in both, the corrective term accounts for the same kinds of margins in both cases and is not affected by the adjustment.[12] The same holds true for products that are exported in both situations. The problem only arises for non-traded goods and for goods suffering trade

---

11. See, for example, Balassa et al. (1971), app. A, p. 324. Another example is Corden (1971), ch. 5.
12. Provided appropriate asssumptions are made regarding the valuation of trade and transport margins within the country.

character changes as a result of the adjustment.

A positive exchange rate adjustment increases the potential import and export prices, measured in domestic currency units. Consequently goods that were imported in the unadjusted free-trade situation may become non-traded or even exported with the adjustment. Similarly, non-traded goods may become exported. It is worth noting that in all these cases the adjustment leads to a reduction in the corrective term. Where an imported product becomes exported the correction even turns from positive to negative.

From the non-standard conversion rule (3.10) it appears that the reduction in the corrective term counteracts the effect of the adjustment term itself. In other words the lowering effect of the adjustment upon the nominal rates of protection is partly absorbed by the change in the corrective term. If the margin between the potential import and export price is of the same order of magnitude as the adjustment, goods that were non-traded in the unadjusted free-trade situation may remain non-traded and with the assumptions adopted in the section 3.3 - both ordinary and net nominal rates disappearing - the effect of the adjustment would be wiped out completely.

3.5   The Nominal Protective Rate of a Basket of Products

3.5.1 Definition

In most protection studies, the determination of the nominal protective rate of a single commodity is only an intermediate step. As the subject of protection is usually a whole industry it often becomes necessary to measure the protection of a basket of different goods, such as the industry's output or different classes of its material inputs. This section explains how nominal protective rates of individual products can be aggregated so as to measure the nominal protection of a basket of products.

The nominal rate of protection of a basket is a weighted average of the nominal protective rates of the constituent goods. The weights should reflect the importance of each of them and the most appropriate way to measure this importance is through their value at free-trade prices. Denoting the nominal protective rate of the basket by w_0 and

those of the individual products within the basket by w_i, the former can
be written as:

(3.11) $w_0 = (\Sigma_i\, x_i^{ft}\, w_i)/\, \Sigma_i\, x_i^{ft}$

where x_i^{ft} is the value of the individual product i in the basket at
free-trade prices.

Writing these values x_i^{ft} as a product of quantities q_i and prices
p_i^{ft}, and remembering the definition of the nominal protective rate
of a product (3.1), the formula (3.11) can be rewritten as follows:

(3.12) $w_0 = \Sigma_i\, q_i\, p_i^{ft}\, w_i\, /\, \Sigma_i\, x_i^{ft} =$

$$= \Sigma_i\, q_i\, (p_i - p_i^{ft})\, /\, x_0^{ft} = (x_0 - x_0^{ft})\, /\, x_0^{ft}$$

where the subscript '0' implies summation over the basket.

Formula (3.12) expresses the nominal protective rate as the extent
to which the value of the basket at protection prices x_0 exceeds its
value at free-trade prices x_0^{ft}. This interpretation is achieved by
choosing the valuation of the weights at free-trade prices. Observe the
similarity with the definition of the nominal protective rate of an
individual product. There the formulation is in terms of prices, but it
could have been in terms of values as well.

Taking free-trade values rather than protection values, as weights
to obtain these properties is obvious, because the nominal rate of
protection is defined with the free-trade price in the denominator of
the quotient. Had nominal protection been defined in terms of protection
prices, the protection values would have been chosen as weights.

It can also be demonstrated that the conversion from ordinary to
net nominal rates according to formulas (3.8) and (3.10) is commutable
with the above described aggregation rule, that is: the net nominal
protective rate of the basket can be obtained either by first
aggregating the rates of the individual products and then converting the
ordinary rate of the aggregate to the net rate, or by first converting
the individual rates to net rates and afterwards aggregating the net

rates. For the standard conversion (3.8) the proof is straightforward, for non-standard conversion according to (3.10) it requires an appropriate definition of the free-trade corrective term $\bar{b}_0$ for the aggregate.

3.5.2 Relation with Price Index Numbers

From its definition (3.11), it is clear that the nominal protective rate of a basket of goods can be interpreted as an index number for the price level of that basket. Formula (3.12) demonstrates that by choosing the free-trade values of the individual commodities as weights, one plus the protective rate of the basket becomes equal to a price index number with the free-trade situation as the base and the protection situation as the current situation.

As long as the basket is not connected with either the free-trade or protection situation, it is not possible to identify the index number as a Laspeyres or a Paasche index. However as the free-trade situation is not observable as a rule, the baskets are usually drawn from the protection situation. Adhering to the interpretation of the free-trade situation as the base, this implies that the price index corresponding to the nominal protective rate can be interpreted as a Paasche index.

As a consequence of the above interpretation, the nominal protective rate w_0 of a basket can be used to convert the valuation of the basket from free-trade to protection prices and vice versa. If the free-trade value of the basket is denoted by x_0^{ft} and the protection value by x_0, it is readily verified from formula (3.12) that:

$$(3.13a) \qquad x_0 = x_0^{ft} (1 + w_0)$$

$$(3.13b) \qquad x_0^{ft} = x_0 / (1 + w_0)$$

That is, protection values are obtained from free-trade values by multiplication with a factor one plus the nominal rate of protection and, similarly, values at free-trade prices are obtained from protection values by division by the same factor.

The connection of the nominal rate of protection with the subject of price index numbers is scarcely taken up in the literature.[13] Here such an interpretation of nominal protection is always waiting in me wings where quantities taken from the protection situation are valued at free-trade prices.

13. An exception is an article written by Koo (1971).

4 Measuring nominal protection

4.1   Measuring Nominal Protection through Tariffs

4.1.1 The Tariff Rate and the Nominal Rate of Protection

In this chapter alternative methods of measuring nominal
protection are discussed. The first section focuses on the measurement
through tariffs. Some implications of the price comparison approach are
then set out, concluding with a section dealing with the possibility of
combining the two forms of measurement.

Turning to the measurement through tariffs, and confining the case
to the importation of goods that are not subject to any quantitative
restrictions, but only to an import tariff or similar price measures: in
that case it is possible to define the nominal rate of protection
directly through the tariff rate without the need to observe domestic
and world market prices. Assuming that competition between imports and
domestic production is perfect, the domestic free-trade price settles at
the c.i.f. price of the imported equivalent and the protection price
becomes equal to the tariff-inclusive import price. As a result, the
nominal rate of protection becomes equal to the tariff rate in ad-
valorem terms.

In most practical cases, however, competition between domestic
production and imports is not perfect. On many occasions quality
differences or brand preferences make domestic consumers prefer the
imported goods to the domestically produced equivalent. It has been
rightly argued by Balassa[1] that in such cases the tariff rate usually
overestimates the upward effect of the tariff upon the price of the
domestically produced goods.

Apart from that, there are also a number of factors complicating
the measurement of the tariff rate itself. First of all the tariff may
be formulated in specific rather than ad-valorem terms. For example, the
import tariff on wines may be 40 pesos per litre. In such cases the
specific rates should be converted to equivalent ad-valorem rates either

1. See Balassa (1971).

by expressing them as a percentage of the import price of the product or
by setting the tariff revenue on the item against its import value. In
that way however part of the advantages of the method - no need for
price observation - is lost.

A similar problem arises when trade flows are under or
overinvoiced for purposes of tax evasion or transfer pricing. In that
case the ad-valorem equivalent of the tariff does not coincide with the
official ad-valorem rate and can only be assessed if the extent of under
or overinvoicing is known. This problem is more serious, first because
it is often difficult to know whether or not such under or overinvoicing
takes place, and secondly because, if it takes place, it is usually
applied to highly differentiated products for which price observation is
complicated.

Another difficulty arises when the country participates in
international-economic-integration agreements with tariff preferences.
In such cases tariffs applicable to trade with integration partners may
be different from those holding for trade with third countries. If so,
the tariff rate with third countries is the one that matters. It must be
realised however that in those circumstances no country can freely
choose to move towards free trade without breaking the integration
conventions.

Still another complication arises when specific importers are
eligible for tariff exemptions or rebates. Then, the marginal tariff
rate, that is, the amount of tariffs to be paid on an extra unit of
imports, is the one that determines the markup of the domestic price.
For that reason the marginal rather than the average rate should be
taken as the protective rate of the product.

In the following the simplifying assumption is made that there is
a uniquely defined ad-valorem equivalent tariff rate t_{imp} on imports and
t_{exp} on exports which does not depend on the origin or destination of
the goods. That is to say that the above-mentioned difficulties are
disregarded. Instead the discussion is focused on a more serious
disadvantage of measuring protection through tariffs, namely the
possibility that the trade character of the product changes with the
elimination of the foreign-trade regime.

Putting the nominal rate of protection equal to the import tariff
rate t_{imp} is only permitted if the goods are indeed imported in both

free-trade and protection situations. In the real world however it frequently happens that import tariffs are prohibitive so that the goods to which they are applicable become non-traded. In that case part of the import tariff is redundant and the tariff rate overestimates the nominal rate of protection of the product concerned. Similarly an export subsidy may cause a product which was previously non-traded to become exported. In that case only part of the export subsidy is needed to cover the difference between the domestic free-trade and the potential export price and the nominal protective rate becomes lower than the subsidy rate. Finally it is possible that certain products that would be exported under free trade become non-traded due to export taxes. If so the export tax rate understates the negative nominal protection.

Where there is no exchange rate adjustment, the above mentioned are the most frequently recurring examples of trade-character changes. If the free-trade exchange rate is considerably different from the existing one the situation becomes more complex. In the following subsections a more systematic discussion is given of trade character changes and of the way in which the relation between the tariff rate and the nominal rate of protection is affected by such changes.

4.1.2 Trade Character Changes: No Exchange Rate Adjustment

In the following it is assumed that the foreign-trade regime exclusively consists of ad-valorem import tariffs at rates t_{imp} and export taxes at rates t_{exp}. The import tariff rates t_{imp} are always positive or zero, but the export tax rate t_{exp} may be negative. In that case, exports are subsidized at a positive rate $s_{exp} = - t_{exp}$. For the moment it is assumed that there is no exchange rate adjustment in the free-trade situation. The latter assumption is relaxed in the next subsection.

Although there is no need for the observation of prices if nominal protection is to be measured through tariffs, in order to illustrate the shortcomings of such an approach it is useful to pay some attention to the unobserved underlying price relations. To that end the following prices are considered:

   i. p   the existing protection price of the goods;
  ii. p_{imp} the (potential) import price at the existing exchange rate;[2]
 iii. p_{exp} the (potential) export price at the existing exchange rate;
  iv. $\tilde{p}_{imp}$ the (potential) tariff-inclusive import price:
$$\tilde{p}_{imp} = p_{imp} (1 + t_{imp})$$
   v. $\tilde{p}_{exp}$ the (potential) export-tax-exclusive (subsidy-inclusive)
            export price: $\tilde{p}_{exp} = p_{exp}(1 - t_{exp}) = p_{exp}(1 + s_{exp})$

To gain some insight into the possible price relations and trace out the
trade character changes that may result from the elimination of the
system of protection, it may be helpful to consider the following
diagram, in which these prices are represented as points on a straight
line.

Diagram 4.1   Trade Character Changes: no exchange rate adjustment

Free-Trade Situation:	exported	non-traded $\tilde{p}_{exp}$		imported $\tilde{p}_{imp}$
Protection Situation:	p_{exp} exported		p_{imp} non-traded	imported

In this diagram it is assumed that there is a positive export subsidy in
force. Should there be an export tax instead, the point $\tilde{p}_{exp}$ would
result on the left side of p_{exp}. Moreover it is assumed that the export
subsidy does not cover the whole range (p_{exp}, p_{imp}). Otherwise the
point $\tilde{p}_{exp}$ would have been on the right of p_{imp}.
       Making similar assumptions on the trade character of the product
in the protection situation as in Chapter 3 for the free-trade
situation, the trade character of the product is defined by the position
of the existing protection price on the straight line in the way it is
indicated in the diagram. That is, whether the product is exported,
imported or non-traded under protection depends on whether its price is
below, above or within the interval $(\tilde{p}_{exp}, \tilde{p}_{imp})$ It should be noted
however that under the assumptions of this section - no quantitative

2. See subsection 3.3.4.

restrictions, just a uniform ad-valorem tariff or subsidy and perfect
competition - not all protection prices are feasible. If the product is
exported in the protection situation, it is assumed that competition
forces its price up to the $\tilde{p}_{exp}$ level. Lower prices would not be
feasible. Similarly, if the product is imported under protection its
price is supposed to be at the $\tilde{p}_{imp}$ level, not higher.

In these circumstances it is clear that with the elimination of
the system of protection an imported product remains imported and
assuming that its free-trade price settles at p_{imp}, nominal protection
equals the import tariff rate $t_{imp} = (\tilde{p}_{imp} - p_{imp})/p_{imp}$ and the tariff
approach predicts nominal protection correctly.

From the diagram it can be seen however that an exported product
may either remain exported or become non-traded. If it remains exported,
its free-trade price settles at p_{exp} and its nominal protection equals
the export subsidy rate $s_{exp} = (\tilde{p}_{exp} - p_{exp})/p_{exp}$. If it becomes non-
traded the free-trade price settles somewhere in the range (p_{exp}, p_{imp})
but most probably on the left of $\tilde{p}_{exp}$ due to the additional supply in
the domestic market of products that were exported under protection.
Thus nominal protection will be in the range between zero and s_{exp}. In
the former case the tariff approach works correctly but in the latter it
overestimates the nominal protective rate.

Finally products that are non-traded in the protection situation
may either become imported or remain non-traded under free trade. The
former case represents the well-known redundancy of import tariffs and
nominal protection results positive but lower than (or at most equal to)
the tariff rate t_{imp}. In the latter case it is difficult to predict
where the free-trade price would settle precisely and it is usually
assumed that nominal protection is zero.[3]

If there is a positive export tax in force the $\tilde{p}_{exp}$ point results
on the left of p_{exp}. Consequently the transition from exportedness under
protection to non-tradedness under free trade is not feasible any more.
Instead it becomes possible that a product that was non-traded in the
protection situation becomes exported on the elimination of the export
tax. In that case nominal protection is at most as negative as the
export tax rate t_{exp}.

3. See subsection 3.3.6.

Not considering the possibility of an export subsidy covering the whole range (p_{exp}, p_{imp}), the above discussed possible combinations are brought together in table 4.1.

It becomes clear that even in the absence of an exchange rate adjustment there is much more to the nominal rate of protection than just the import and export tariff rates. Particularly, non-tradedness of goods which would be imported under free trade is a frequently recurring phenomenon which causes discrepancies between the nominal rate of protection, on the one hand, and the tariff rate on the other.

Table 4.1   The Nominal Rate of Protection: no exchange rate adjustment

Free Trade:	Imported	Non-traded	Exported
Protection:			
Imported	t_{imp}	(excl.)	(excl.)
Non-Traded	(0, t_{imp})	0	($- t_{exp}$, 0)[*]
Exported	(excl.)	(0, s_{exp})[**]	$- t_{exp} = s_{exp}$

[*] Only if t_{exp} is positive.
[**] Only if s_{exp} is positive.

4.1.3 Trade Character Changes under Exchange Rate Adjustment

If the exchange rate is adjusted to the free-trade conditions the situation becomes even more complex. On one hand the elimination of the tariffs has a downward effect upon the prices of products competing with imports, but on the other there is an upward effect resulting from the exchange rate adjustment, at least if the latter consists of a devaluation, which is usually the case. The net effect is described by the adjusted import tariff rate $\bar{t}_{imp}$ which is defined as:

$$(4.1) \qquad \bar{t}_{imp} = \frac{1 + t_{imp}}{1 + \phi} - 1 = \frac{1}{1 + \phi} (t_{imp} - \phi)$$

where ϕ stands for the magnitude of the adjustment.

Throughout the following it is assumed that the adjustment is positive, that is, the free-trade exchange rate is devalued in

comparison with the existing one. In principle negative adjustments are
conceivable, but as most foreign-trade regimes are more restrictive on
the import than on the export side (if at all restrictive on the export
side), this phenomenon is not likely to occur.

It is interesting to note the similarity between formula (4.1) for
the conversion of the normal to the adjusted import tariff rate, and the
standard conversion rule (3.8) for nominal protection.It is readily
verified that the adjusted import tariff rate can be considered as the
relative extent to which the domestic currency costs of a unit of
imports in the protection situation exceed those in the adjusted free-
trade situation.

Similarly <u>adjusted export tax (subsidy) rate</u> is defined as:

$$(4.2) \qquad \bar{t}_{exp} = \frac{t_{exp} - 1}{1 + \phi} + 1 = \frac{1}{1 + \phi} \, (t_{exp} + \phi)$$

In contrast with the adjusted import tariff rate of equation (4.1), here
the export tax and the exchange rate adjustment work in the same
direction because both export tax and overvaluation discriminate against
exports. A similar economic interpretation can be given to the adjusted
export tax rate $\bar{t}_{exp}$. It is the relative extent to which domestic
currency receipts for a unit of exports fall short of those that would
have been made in the adjusted free-trade situation.

The unobserved prices underlying the possible trade character
changes in the presence of an exchange rate adjustment are now:

p   the existing protection price of the goods (as before);

$\bar{p}_{imp}$ the potential import price at the adjusted exchange rate:

        i.e. $\bar{p}_{imp} = (1 + \phi) \, p_{imp}$;

$\bar{p}_{exp}$ the potential export price at the adjusted exchange rate:

        i.e. $\bar{p}_{exp} = (1 + \phi) \, p_{exp}$;

$\tilde{p}_{imp}$ the (potential) tariff-inclusive import price,

        i.e. $\tilde{p}_{imp} = p_{imp}(1 + t_{imp}) = \bar{p}_{imp}(1 + \bar{t}_{imp})$;

$\tilde{p}_{exp}$ the (potential) export-tax-exclusive (subsidy-inclusive)
export

        price, i.e. $\tilde{p}_{exp} = p_{exp}(1 - t_{exp}) = \bar{p}_{exp}(1 - \bar{t}_{exp})$.

Comparing these prices with those considered in section 4.1.2, only the potential export and import prices p_{imp} and p_{exp} have been adjusted to $\bar{p}_{imp}$ and $\bar{p}_{exp}$ to account for the exchange rate adjustment. As the tariff-corrected prices $\tilde{p}_{imp}$ and $\tilde{p}_{exp}$ refer to the protection situation they remain unaffected.

The possible occurrence of certain trade character transitions now depends on the magnitude of the adjustment in comparison with the applicable tariffs. The following price diagram gives an example:

Diagram 4.2 Trade Character Changes under Exchange Rate Adjustment

Free-Trade Situation:	exported		non-traded		imported	
	$\tilde{p}_{exp}$				$\tilde{p}_{imp}$	
Protection Situation:	p_{exp}	$\bar{p}_{exp}$	p_{imp}	$\bar{p}_{imp}$		
	exported		non-traded		imported	

In this diagram it is assumed that the exchange rate adjustment is smaller than the unadjusted import tariff rate so that the adjusted price $\bar{p}_{imp}$ remains on the same side of $\tilde{p}_{imp}$ as the unadjusted price p_{imp}. Consequently products that are imported in the protection situation remain imported in the adjusted free-trade situation and their nominal protection equals the adjusted import tariff rate $\bar{t}_{imp}$. If the existing protection price falls in the $(\bar{p}_{imp}, \tilde{p}_{imp})$ interval, the product is non-traded under protection but becomes imported in the free-trade situation. In that case nominal protection is positive, but at most equal to $\bar{t}_{imp}$.

On the export side however there is a change of position. While the unadjusted price p_{exp} was on the left side of $\tilde{p}_{exp}$, the adjusted price $\bar{p}_{exp}$ is on the right side. This implies that the devaluation of the currency to the free-trade situation represents a stronger export incentive than the original export subsidy. As a consequence, if the product is exported under protection, it definitely remains exported under free-trade and if the product is non-traded in the protection situation with a price in the $(\tilde{p}_{exp}, \bar{p}_{exp})$ interval, it becomes exported. In the former case the net nominal protective rate is equal to the adjusted subsidy rate $\bar{s}_{exp} = -\bar{t}_{exp}$ which can be shown to be negative. In the latter, net nominal protection also results negative but less negative than (or at most as negative as) $\bar{s}_{exp}$.

Let us now consider the case of a product with an export subsidy
rate larger than the exchange rate adjustment and no import tariff. This
case is visualised by the following diagram:

Diagram 4.3   Trade Character Changes under Exchange Rate Adjustment

Free Trade	exported		non-traded		imported
Situation:		$\tilde{p}_{exp}$		$\tilde{p}_{imp}$	
Protection	p_{exp}	p_{exp}		p_{imp}	p_{imp}
Situation:		exported	non-traded	imported	

If the product is exported in both situations a similar reasoning leads
to a nominal protective rate equal to the adjusted subsidy
rate $\bar{s}_{exp}$ which is now positive. Should the product be imported, nominal
protection would become negative and equal to the adjusted import tariff
rate $\bar{t}_{imp} = -\phi$. There is a possibility however that the product, if it
was traded in the protection situation, becomes non-traded under free
trade. If it was exported under protection, previously exported supply
would turn to the domestic market and the free-trade price would settle
at a lower level. In this way the nominal rate of protection would be
positive but at most equal to $\bar{s}_{exp}$. Similarly if the product was
imported, then lost supply from abroad would lead to a higher price in
the domestic market under free trade and nominal protection would be
negative with $\bar{t}_{imp}$ as a lower limit.

Again disregarding the possibility of complete trade reversals,
the above indicated cases are brought together in the Table 4.2. The
scheme shows a marked resemblance to Table 4.1, but all tariff rates are
adjusted. Moreover certain transitions that were excluded in Table 4.1
are now feasible. Generally there is an enhanced tendency towards
exportation in the free-trade situation.

Table 4.2 The Nominal Rate of Protection: with exchange rate adjustment

Free Trade:	Imported	Non-Traded	Exported
Protection:			
Imported	$\bar{t}_{imp}$	$(\ \bar{t}_{imp},\ 0\ )^{1}$	(excl.)
Non-traded	$(\ 0,\ \bar{t}_{imp})^{2}$	0	$(\ -\bar{t}_{exp},\ 0\ )^{3}$
Exported	(excl.)	$(0,\ -\bar{t}_{exp})^{4}$	$-\bar{t}_{exp}$

1. Only possible if $\bar{t}_{imp}$ is negative.
2. Only possible if t_{imp} is positive.
3. Only possible if $\bar{t}_{exp}$ is positive.
4. Only possible if $\bar{t}_{exp}$ is negative.

4.1.4 The Tariff Rate and Nominal Protection: Concluding Remarks

From the foregoing it may be concluded that generally the tariff rate itself tends to overestimate its impact on domestic prices. That is the case not only if as a result of quality differences, brand preferences, and so on, competition between imports and domestic production is less than perfect, but also if with the elimination of the foreign-trade regime the trade character of the goods changes. In Tables 4.1 and 4.2 such trade character changes are represented by the off-diagonal entries. There it is invariably shown that in absolute terms the nominal protective rate is at most equal to, but as a rule smaller than the tariff rate. In other words if the tariff leads to positive protection, the real nominal protection is indeed positive (or zero) but usually smaller than the tariff rate itself (adjusted or unadjusted). If on the other hand the tariff leads to negative protection either due to export taxation or as a result of the exchange rate adjustment, the nominal protective rate is indeed negative (or zero) but usually not as negative as the tariff rate would suggest.

Altogether it is clear that the mere fact that a product's imports or exports are not subject to any quantitative restrictions far from guarantees that its nominal protection is correctly measured by the tariff rate. On the contrary, the tariff approach, even in its more sophisticated forms, tends to overestimate the real impact on domestic price levels and thus the nominal protective rate in absolute terms.

4.2   Measuring Nominal Protection through Price Comparison

4.2.1 General Remarks

As soon as there are quantitative restrictions in force, such as import or export quota regulations or licensing, the tariff approach to the measurement of nominal protection breaks down completely. Such quantitative restrictions may cause domestic prices to diverge from world market quotations even in the absence of tariffs so that nominal protection can only be measured by comparing domestic prices directly with international quotations.

The key problem in this field is to establish the sample of goods for which price comparisons should be made. In the tariff approach this problem hardly exists. There the problem is rather to classify the goods that constitute the basket for which nominal protection is measured according to the tariff code. But for purposes of price comparison the classification of such tariff codes is still too aggregated as a rule.

In order to be priceable a product must be very specific. The level of specification of, for example, 'iron nails' is not sufficient. To assign them a more or less well-defined price per pound it will be necessary also to specify their length, to indicate whether or not they are galvanised, and so on. But at such levels of specification there are easily some ten million different products to be distinguished in any somewhat diversified economy. Thus if the aim is to measure nominal protection for the production of all sectors of an economy, the work must be done on a sampling basis.

In the following it is assumed that the objective is to measure the nominal protection of the production of a sector during a certain year. The value of production at protection prices is denoted by the symbol x. In the production accounts of the sector, production is classified according to some generic classification, which is not detailed enough to come to proper price comparisons but coincides to a certain extent with the classification of the tariff lists. Should the sector be that of metal products, iron nails might appear as one of the generic products on the list. It is assumed that for these generic products both production value x_i and production volume (in metric tons, cubic metres, pieces or otherwise) q_i is given. Consequently a unit value for any of these generic products can be obtained by division:

(4.3) $p_i^{unit} = x_i / q_i$

The value of production for the sector as a whole is supposed to be the sum of the production values of the constituent generic products:

(4.4) $x_0 = \Sigma_i \, x_i$

Similarly the generic products can be divided into priceable items indicated by an extra subscript on the symbols:

(4.5) $p_{ij} = x_{ij} / q_{ij}$

(4.6) $x_i = \Sigma_j \, x_{ij}$

Bearing in mind that where information on value and volume of production is still available at the generic level, at the priceable level the same information cannot be disposed as a rule. Generally the identification of products at the priceable level is already problematic. As a consequence, x_{ij} and q_{ij} are usually not known and the average price p_{ij} of production over the period must be approximated by market quotations or by the price at which certain transactions took place.

4.2.2 The Sample

As the number of priceable items in the production of a sector is usually very large, it is impossible to make price comparisons for all of them. Instead nominal protection must be measured on a sample, though to establish a representative sample is far from easy. It is mainly complicated by the fact that for many products at the priceable level the measurement of nominal protection often turns out unfeasible. For that reason some observations about the measurability of nominal protection would be in order.

Before an individual product at the priceable level can be included in the sample its nominal rate of protection must be measured through price comparison. To that end the following rather obvious conditions must be met:

i. the product must be identified;

ii. its average price of production p_{ij} must be estimated either by market quotations or by transaction prices;

iii. the same product must be identified in the international market or in international transactions;

iv. its international price π_{ij} must be detected;

v. additional information must be available on trade and transport margins.

However obvious they may be, these conditions are not easily fulfilled simultaneously. In particular, condition (iii) is not easily combined with condition (i), and the more detailed the level of specification of the product, the more difficult it will be to find identical counterproducts in international transactions. Moreover prices in both domestic and international transactions may show so much variation that price comparisons become meaningless. Therefore those products must be excluded from the sample for it is impossible to measure their nominal protective rates.

In the circumstances it is virtually impossible to establish a random sample. The condition of measurability of nominal protection introduces a bias which easily leads to overrepresentation of certain products and underrepresentation of others. Exported products, for example, may become overrepresented as a result of the relative easiness to identify equivalent counterproducts in international transactions. Highly differentiated products however may easily become underrepresented due to problems of product identification and price estimation.

This bias would not be so serious if there were not strong reasons to believe that nominal protection for exported goods is systematically lower than that for the non-traded tradables and imported goods. Similarly it is quite possible that nominal protection of highly differentiated products is higher, on an average, than that of the more homogeneous goods. Altogether nominal protection estimates tend to be biased downwards if no proper attention is given to the selection of products in the sample.

These sceptical remarks on establishing a fully representative sample are not intended to discourage. They should be taken as an appeal to be realistic and try to improve the representativeness of the sample. To do that an attempt should be made to define generic products in such a way that there is little variation of nominal protection among the constituent priceable items of each generic product. If that is successful a reasonable estimate of the nominal rate of protection for the whole sector would be obtained by taking one or just a few priceable items within each generic product, then assigning the (average) nominal rate of the items to the corresponding generic product and finally aggregating the nominal rates according to formula (3.11).

In fact full representativeness of the sample is guaranteed if (i) intra-generic variation of protection is zero, and (ii) each generic product is represented by at least one priceable subproduct. If the latter condition is not met, it is rather obvious that those generic products which take a large share in the sectoral production value should be represented first. If one of them is missing, it is worse than the absence of one with a lower participation. With respect to the first condition, it should be remembered that the higher the intra-generic variation, the more it pays to extend the number of subproducts and to estimate their production value x_{ij} in order to make a weighting of the rates of the subproducts possible.

4.2.3 Price Comparisons at the Priceable Level

In the process of comparing domestic with world market prices, the difficulties to be faced are similar to those encountered with intertemporal price comparisons in the elaboration of price index numbers.[4] Most of these arise from the fact that detected price differences can be due to different factors other than the trade regime or, in the case of price deflators, than the time elapsed. The most important of the other factors causing price differences are the following.

Specification Differences. Even at the priceable level it may happen that there are still differences in the characteristics of domestically produced and internationally traded varieties. It could be argued obviously that the level of specification was not sufficient, but it should be borne in mind that the more detailed the level of

4. For a discussion of the main difficulties see Allen (1975), ch. 7.

specification, the more difficult it becomes to find internationally traded equivalents to the domestically produced goods. Moreover some products, for example, ships are unique, which makes proper price comparisons virtually impossible. It should also be observed that all these difficulties are less serious in the case of intertemporal price comparisons. Generally it is much easier to find identical products at different times because most of them are produced to standard specifications by the same producers and often by the same machines. With international price comparisons however there is much less guarantee that products of international transactions are identical to those of domestic origin.

Quality Differences. Similar observations can be made with respect to quality differences. Often importation of certain goods takes place precisely because the domestically produced equivalent is of a lower quality, and in the same way it is usually only the best part of domestic production that qualifies for exportation. This phenomenon tends to bias nominal protection downwards if no appropriate allowance is made for quality differences. With the elaboration of intertemporal price index numbers there is a similar problem. There technological innovations may lead to new products or products of improved quality, which make their comparability with older products doubtful.

Trade and Transport Margins.[5] This is another source of price differentials which cannot be attributed to the foreign-trade regime. Again it is easier to observe prices at equivalent points in the trade and transport chain at different periods than among domestically produced and internationally traded varieties.

Seasonal Variations. If nominal protection is measured not for a single transaction but for all transactions during a whole year, seasonal fluctuations of prices may bias the outcome considerably. For certain products, particularly fruit and vegetables, domestic prices may fluctuate so heavily over the period that it is more difficult to make reliable estimates of the nominal protective rate through price comparisons.

Under and Overinvoicing. For the purpose of tax evasion transactions are often under or overinvoiced. In such cases it is hardly

5. See also subsection 3.3.4.

possible to disclose the proper prices at which the transactions took place, and differences in declared prices stemming from such practices might be wrongly ascribed to the foreign-trade regime.

Transfer Pricing. Transactions between different subsidiaries of transnational enterprises are often valued at artificially high or low prices in order to transfer profits from one country to another with a softer tax regime. This is not the same phenomenon as under or overinvoicing, because here the amount invoiced is also paid. Consequently the declared price is the real price, but the real price does not represent free-trade market conditions and should be avoided for the purpose of price comparison.

Industrial and Commercial Relations. The price charged by a producer for a certain product may depend on the regularity of the demand of the purchaser. Special relations among firms may cause certain transactions to be valued at prices far different from market quotations. For some products, for example, a number of intermediate chemicals, this is so common a practice that market quotations do not make much sense. In fact all sorts of price discriminations fall into this category.

A special frequently recurring case of market imperfections is that of manufactured exports, particularly manufactured products with a low raw material content. Domestic producers who sell these products domestically under imperfect market conditions usually export the same product at somewhat lower prices even if no export subsidies are applicable. According to Balassa[6], 'cartellized producers sell at marginal costs abroad and charge in the protected domestic market a price that includes allowance for fixed costs on their entire output'. In such cases nominal protection for that part of production which is sold on the domestic market comes out positive if it is measured by price comparison. Should the nominal protective rate be measured by the subsidy rate, however, it would be zero.

Which of the two rates is the correct measure for nominal protection - the tariff (subsidy) rate or the price comparison rate - depends on what is assumed in the free-trade situation. If the same policies of price discrimination are supposed to persist under free-

6. See Balassa (1971).

trade conditions, the tariff rate is the one to be selected. But if it is assumed that market conditions become perfect under free trade, the price comparison rate should be taken.

In this study the latter assumption is adhered to. This implies that the nominal protective rate resulting from price comparisons is the correct rate by assumption. The tariff rate can only be used as a stand-by in cases where tariff rates are more easily obtained.

4.2.4 Price Comparisons at the Generic Level

Instead of comparing transaction prices or market prices at the priceable level, it is also possible to compare unit values at the generic level. One example would be to set the unit value of domestic production of iron nails per pound against the unit value of the same item on the import bill.

Needless to say, this procedure may introduce a number of unverifiable biases. Imported varieties may be of different characteristics and quality from the domestically produced goods. That is particularly likely to occur in countries with import substitution policies where only those items are given entrance to the country that do not really compete with domestic production. For that reason it is often preferable to resort to the foreign-trade statistics of other countries rather than those of the country concerned, but there is still little guarantee that the goods compared would be identical.

Besides that, even if the goods in the domestic and international baskets are reasonably comparable, there may be differences in the composition of the basket. Higher-priced items, for example, may have a larger share in the international than in the domestic basket or vice versa. Likewise the bulk of international transactions may have taken place during a short period not representative of the full period. If so, differences in unit value, which in reality are due to differences in quality, composition and timing, are wrongly attributed to the foreign-trade regime.

For these reasons most theorists in the field seem to agree on the absolute superiority of comparisons at the priceable level and categorically reject unit value comparisons at the generic level. Yet the priceable level is often so difficult to reach that many practitioners resort mainly to the generic level, with a few exceptions where the generic level comprises products of so heterogeneous a character that unit value comparisons would become meaningless.

Apart from the evident practical reasons, there are also theoretical arguments that can be brought up in defence of unit value comparisons at the generic level. First there is usually much more variation of prices at the priceable level. Prices may vary from day to day, from one place to another, from one transaction to another and, depending on the item involved, these fluctuations may be considerable. At the generic level there is some sort of implicit averaging which, however biased it may be, excludes the risk of picking out a price on the edge of the variation interval. Secondly working at the generic level raises no problems in respect of the representativeness of the items within the generic product as a whole. At the priceable level the risk exists that items are selected with nominal rates of protection far away from the average. The only way to control these phenomena would be to carry out a fully-fledged analysis of variance for each selected item but this usually goes far beyond the scope of any protection study.

Altogether the conclusion that the best procedure is a combination of both methods seems to be justified. For practical reasons working at the generic level is better but whenever the generic product is too heterogeneous, turning to the priceable level cannot be avoided.

4.3 Combining the Price Comparison Approach with the Tariff Approach

4.3.1 General Remarks

The discussion of section 4.2 demonstrates that it is much easier to measure nominal protection through tariffs than through price comparisons. But in most foreign-trade regimes, particularly those of developing countries, quantitative restrictions play an important role and the price comparison approach is usually the only option available. None the less the mere presence of quantitative restrictions does not imply that the tariff system would no longer contain information relevant to the measurement of nominal protection. On the contrary, in this section it is shown that information on tariffs and on the trade character of the products can be used as a rough check on the significance of price comparisons. Moreover information on tariffs is needed to assess the so-called premium to the licenceholder, that is the difference between the domestic value of goods imported under licence and the tariff-inclusive import value.

Throughout the following it is generally assumed that there is no adjustment of the exchange rate to the free-trade situation. Wherever applicable the generalisation to cover an exchange rate adjustment is straightforward.

4.3.2 Compatibility

In the process of comparing prices it is often found that for certain imported products c.i.f. import prices are higher than the domestic prices of equivalent products of domestic origin even under a heavily restrictive regime. Consequently the price comparison approach would lead to a negative nominal rate of protection for those products. Evidently such price differences cannot be ascribed to the foreign-trade regime, but should rather be attributed to quality differences, brand preferences and so on In order to avoid such spurious comparisons, a check with the trade character of the product and the applicable tariff may be useful.

The following exposition is subdivided according to the trade character of the product in the protection situation. In every case a permitted range for the nominal protective rate is derived depending on the applicable tariff and whether or not quantitative restrictions apply. Compatibility then implies that any price comparison leading to a nominal protective rate outside that range is rejected.

Imported Goods. For imported goods ordinary nominal protection - that is, without exchange rate adjustment - cannot conceivably be negative as long as the government does not actively stimulate importation, which is seldom the case. If an import tariff t_{imp} (measured in ad-valorem terms) is applicable it should be positive and of the same magnitude as t_{imp}. If on top of that quantitative restrictions are in force, the nominal protective rate may still be higher and t_{imp} should be considered as a lower limit. Upper limits cannot a priori be given in that case.

Exported Goods. Exported goods may be positively or negatively protected depending on whether their exportation is stimulated by subsidies or hampered by export taxes. If exportation is taxed with an export tax t_{exp}, nominal protection is negative and of the same magnitude as t_{exp}. If exports are subsidised with a positive export subsidy $s_{exp} = -t_{exp}$, nominal protection is positive and equal to s_{exp}. If besides the tax or subsidy exportation is subject to licensing, the indicated values represent upper limits to the nominal protective rate. Lower limits cannot a priori be given.

An exception should be made for the case of manufactured exports with a low raw material content. In section 4.2 it was argued that these products are often exported at prices lower than those charged in the protected domestic market. However price differences between domestic and export markets are not all that high (10 to 15 per cent) as a rule. All the same it is reasonable to allow for such positive protection of manufactured goods by not putting the upper limit to the nominal protective rate at zero, but at +15 per cent in the absence of an export subsidy or if this subsidy is lower.

Non-Traded Goods. For the non-traded goods, it would be interesting to know whether or not they would be traded in the free-trade situation and if so, in which direction. Following the assumptions set out in subsection 3.3.5, it is the price relation that defines the trade character under free-trade conditions. In this section however the price relation is subjected to doubt and cannot be used for that purpose. But it is possible to indicate an allowed range for the nominal protective rate, at least if there are no quantitative restrictions in force. The lower limit is defined by minus the export tax rate t_{exp}, which is positive in case of a subsidy, and the upper limit is rated equal to the import tariff rate. As soon as quantitative restrictions enter in force the lower limit is relaxed if these restrictions apply to exports and the upper limit if they apply to imports.

In Table 4.3 the allowed ranges for the nominal protective rate are given schematically from case to case. The limits should not be taken too strictly. A price comparison leading to a nominal protective rate far outside the indicated interval should definitely be rejected. But if the nominal protective rate resulting from a price comparison is just outside the allowed range it can be accepted, although it is preferable in that case to put nominal protection equal to the value of the closest limit.

Consider, for example, the case of an imported product subject to a tariff of 30 per cent ad-valorem and to import licensing. If a price comparison should lead to a nominal rate of 25 per cent, this rate would be outside the permitted range of 30 per cent or higher. It still seems reasonable to accept the underlying price comparison. But nominal protection is more likely to be 30 than 25 per cent.

Table 4.3 Allowed Ranges for the Nominal Rate of Protection

Trade Character and Regime	Lower Limit	Upper Limit
Imported Goods		
Import Tariff only	t_{imp}	t_{imp}
Also Quant. Restrictions	t_{imp}	none
Exported Goods		
Export Tax only[1]	$-t_{exp}$	$-t_{exp}$[2]
Also Quant. Restrictions	none	$-t_{exp}$[2]
Non-Traded Goods		
Only Price Measures[3]	$-t_{exp}$	t_{imp}
Quant. Restr. on Imports	$-t_{exp}$	none
Quant. Restr. on Exports	none	t_{imp}
Quant. Restr. on both	none	none

1. This case also includes the export subsidy. In that case t_{exp} is negative.
2. Upper limits may be put somewhat higher for manufactured goods with low raw material content. See the explanation in the text.
3. For simplicity's sake it is assumed that these are just import tariffs and export taxes. As in the other cases, other price measures can be translated into a tariff equivalent.

In this way it is possible to set any price comparison found against the applicable trade regime and accept it only in case of compatibility. To that end it is necessary first to define the trade character of the product involved, and then to look for the import tariff, export tax (subsidy) or both depending whether the product is imported, exported or non-traded, respectively. Then it should be checked to see if the price comparison leads to a nominal protective

rate within the permitted interval. If it does the price comparison is
accepted and the nominal protective rate is defined accordingly. If not
the price comparison is rejected. However if it is reasonably close to
the permitted interval it is accepted but the closest limit is
substituted for the rate following from the price comparison.

It should be noted that the above procedure prefers the tariff
rate to the price comparison rate for traded products which are not
subject to quantitative restrictions, in which case the permitted
interval shrinks to the point defined by the tariff rate. Then the price
comparison only serves as a check to see if the price relation is more
or less in accordance with the tariff.

4.3.3 Quantitative Restrictions versus Equivalent Tariffs

If the domestic price of goods imported under licence is higher
than the tariff-inclusive import price, the difference implicitly
accrues to the licenceholder. Denoting the c.i.f. value of the imports
by m, the premium to the licenceholder can be written as follows:

$$(4.7) \qquad h_m = m \, (w - t_{imp})$$

where the nominal rate of protection w cannot be smaller than the tariff
rate t_{imp}. Otherwise the goods would not be imported according to the
assumptions of subsection 3.3.5 and the definition of the nominal
protective rate set out before.

As regards the importation of goods for intermediate consumption,
it may be important to know whether the licence is obtained by a trading
company or direct by the consumer industry itself. This is of particular
interest for the calculation of the effective rates of protection which
is taken up in the Chapter 5.

In a similar way there is a premium to the export licenceholder.
In principle, export licensing causes domestic prices to be lower than
the subsidy-inclusive (or export-tax-exclusive) export price. Again the
resulting revenue difference is the premium to the licenceholder.
Denoting the value of exports by e, this premium can be written as:

$$(4.8) \qquad h_e = - \, e \, (w + t_{exp})$$

where the usually negative nominal protective rate outweighs the export tax rate t_{exp} so that the premium is always positive.

The premiums to the licenceholders are often conceived as potential revenues forgone by the government. If licences are to be substituted by their tariff equivalents - that is, import tariffs or export taxes leading to the same price distortions in the domestic market - the premiums would be siphoned over to the government tax collector. Apart from the evident susceptibility of licensing systems to corruption, the reducing effect on tax revenue is often used as an argument against quantitative restrictions in general.

In this context it is surprising that so little, if any, attention has been paid to the advantages of quantitative restrictions over equivalent tariff systems. World market prices for many commodities fluctuate heavily over a period. With liberalised[7] trade regimes such fluctuations would be transferred direct to the domestic markets. Quantitative restrictions may function instead as shock absorbers allowing domestic prices to remain more or less stable. In that case the premiums to the licenceholders would absorb the fluctuations of international prices.

It may be argued that the same stabilising effect could be achieved by varying the tariff rates with changes in international quotations as done with the EEC system of variable levies on agricultural and food products. However such a system is far from easy to administer and can only be set up for relatively homogeneous products for which regular world market quotations are available.

4.3.4 Precision of Measurement

From the foregoing expositions it has become clear that the measurement of nominal protection is subject to a great number of imitations. The relatively smooth tariff approach can only be used for liberalised trade regimes, that is regimes in which no quantitative restrictions are operative. But even then the tariff approach may lead to incorrect estimates of nominal protection as a result of non-tradedness of tradables and trade character transitions between the

7. The expression 'liberalised trade regime' is used to indicate a regime with price measures only, that is, without quantitative restrictions.

protection and the free-trade situation.

The price comparison approach, on the other hand, faces the same difficulties as those encountered with the elaboration of intertemporal price index numbers. To make it worse, these difficulties - quality differences, matching of incomparable products, price detection, sampling and so on - appear to be even more serious in the field of international price comparisons for the measurement of nominal protection than that of intertemporal price indices.

The compatibility of the price comparisons with the foreign-trade regime here proposed only serves as a rough filter to reject evidently false price comparisons from the sample. It can hardly be expected to guarantee refined nominal protection estimates.

Altogether it would be an illusion to believe that nominal protection could be measured with a high degree of accuracy. On the contrary margins of error are usually substantial. There can be few products where they are in the order of 1 per cent (on both sides); for most products it would be more realistic to consider intervals of 2 to 5 per cent and for still a notable number of products even those margins are too narrow.

At the aggregate sector level the picture is somewhat more optimistic. In the process of aggregation it may be assumed that, to a certain extent, errors for some products cancel out those of others. But even at the sector level the margins of error for nominal protection estimates are believed to remain in the order of magnitude of a few per cent on both sides.

5 Effective protection

5.1 The Effective Rate of Protection

5.1.1 Historical Background

Effective protection does not only consider the protection given to an industry through the relative price increase of its output - as nominal protection does - but takes explicit account of the negative protection due to price increases of its intermediate inputs. In this way protection is no longer measured in terms of the prices of the goods produced but of the value-added generated during their production.

To give an example, let us consider an assembling plant which produces a passenger car at a price of 450 000 pesos. The same car could have been imported under free trade for 300 000 pesos. Thus nominal protection is 50 per cent. Assume that the intermediate inputs required for the production of the car are worth 260 000 pesos at protection prices, but at free-trade prices only 200 000 pesos. Thus nominal protection on the intermediate inputs is 30 per cent. Comparing a value added of 190 000 pesos in the protection situation with a value-added of 100 000 pesos at free-trade prices leads to an effective protection of 90 per cent in this case.

Although it has long been recognised that import tariffs on an intermediate input reduce protection for the consumer industry, it is only a quarter of a century since the concept of effective protection as we know it today was introduced.[1] In 1955 Meade, in his essays on trade and welfare, elaborated an arithmetic exercise in which the effective rate of protection was clearly set out.[2]

The effective rate of protection applies to a productive sector, a productive activity or just a firm. It can be calculated as soon as the intermediate-input cost structure is known and nominal rates of protection are available for all outputs and intermediate inputs. As one specific commodity may serve as an intermediate input to various consumer industries, there may be some economy in calculating effective

1. For a history see Corden (1971), pp. 245-9.
2. See Meade (1955), vol. II, p. 157.

protection for many industries at the same time. In particular, if an
input-output table is available effective protection can be calculated
on an economy-wide basis.

Such economy-wide calculations were first carried out in the mid-
sixties by Soligo and Stern[3] for Pakistan, and by Balassa[4] for a number
of industrialised countries. These pioneering empirical studies were
followed by a large number of practical exercises, among which should be
specially mentioned the intercountry study directed by Balassa[5] and
another by Bhagwati and Krueger.[6] Although there are minor conceptual
differences from one study to another in respect of the treatment of
non-tradable goods, technology adjustment to the free-trade situation,
and so on, the core concept of effective protection is the same in all
studies. A theoretical description of the effective protective rate can
be found, among others, in Corden's work, The Theory of Protection[7].

5.1.2 Definition

The definition of the effective rate of protection is similar to
that of the nominal rate. The difference is that where the nominal rate
applies to goods, the effective rate of protection applies to economic
activities producing them and while nominal protection is defined in
terms of the prices of the goods, effective protection refers to the
value-added generated during their production.

The effective rate of protection of an economic activity is defined
as the percentage by which the value-added (at factor costs) generated
by that activity in the protection situation exceeds the hypothetical
value- added which would have been obtained in the free-trade situation,
that is:

$$(5.1) \qquad z = \frac{y - y^{ft}}{y^{ft}} = \frac{g}{y^{ft}}$$

where y   stands for the value-added at factor costs in the protection

3. See Soligo and Stern (1965).
4. See Balassa (1965).
5. The results are published in Balassa et al. (1971).
6. This research was sponsored by the American National Bureau of
   Economic Research and published in a Special Series on
   Foreign Trade Regimes and Economic Development. See for example
   the summary vols by Krueger (1978) and Bhagwati (1978).
7. See Corden (1971), ch. 3.

situation;

y^{ft} for the value added at free-trade prices;

g   for the effective protection in absolute terms $(y-y^{ft})$ as
     against the effective rate z which expresses effective
     protection in relative terms.

In this definition it is implicitly understood that the package of goods produced in the free-trade situation is the same as in reality. The technology of production however is allowed to vary.

Generally the concept of effective protection as introduced above does not apply to individual goods. It is only if the price of a specific product can be decomposed unequivocally in value-added and intermediate-input shares that effective protection may refer to goods. But given that most economic activities, even at their most disaggregated levels, produce much more than a single priceable item, and that the cost structure is only known for the activity as a whole, it is preferable to relate the concept of effective protection not to goods but to economic activities.

5.1.3 Z-Measure versus U-Measure

By definition (5.1) it is the value-added at free-trade prices that appears in the denominator. However in some early empirical studies of protection[8] effective protection in absolute terms is not related to the value-added at free-trade prices but to the protection value-added. The definition of effective protection changes accordingly to:

$$(5.2) \qquad u = \frac{y - y^{ft}}{y} = \frac{g}{y}$$

This so-called u-measure of effective protection can be interpreted as that part of the value added obtained in the protection situation that can be attributed to the system of protection.

Apart from this directly appealing interpretation, the u-measure has two other advantages over the z-measure. In the first place the value-added gain resulting from protection is no longer related to a

---

8. The study by Lewis and Guisinger (1968) on Pakistan may serve as an
   example.

hypothetical concept (value-added at free-trade prices) as in the z-measure, but to a quantity that is observable in reality. Secondly the z-measure has the disadvantage of a singularity. That is, if the value added at free-trade prices becomes very small or even goes from zero to negative - which happens whenever intermediate input costs become larger than output revenues at free-trade prices - the z-measure first increases disproportionately to infinity, then jumps to minus infinity and remains negative for negative values of the value-added at free-trade prices. However in spite of the negative value of the z-measure the case is one of very strong positive protection. The u-measure on the other hand has no such singularity.

It is worth mentioning that there is no substantial controversy at stake for using one measure or the other. There is a direct algebraic conversion from the u-measure to the z-measure and vice versa:

$$(5.3a, b) \qquad z = \frac{u}{1 - u} \quad \text{and} \quad u = \frac{z}{1 + z}$$

Therefore there is no strong reason to advocate the use of the u-measure instead of the z-measure. Moreover in the vast literature on the subject the z-measure seems to have won the game. And in the following the z-measure is adopted.

5.2   Estimating the Value-Added at Free-Trade Prices

5.2.1 Value-Added in the Protection Situation

In the following, the expression 'buyers' prices' is used for prices paid by the buyers. Producers' prices are buyers' prices net of trade and transport margins. Basic prices are producers' prices net of commodity taxes. The term 'factor prices' is only applied to value-added and indicates that non-commodity taxes are also excluded.

In general terms the value added at factor prices generated by an activity is the value of its output at basic prices minus the value of its intermediate inputs at buyers' prices minus non-commodity taxes. This can be denoted in the following way:

$$(5.4) \qquad y = \Sigma_k q_k p_k + \Sigma_\ell e_\ell p_\ell^e - \Sigma_i a_i p_i - \Sigma_j m_j p_j^m - TT - TC - TN - TI - TE$$

where y is the value-added at factor prices obtained by the activity;

q_k the volume of product k produced by the activity for the
domestic market;

e_ℓ the volume of product b produced for the export market;

p_k the basic price received by the producer on domestic sales of
product k;

p_ℓ^e the price, including export taxes and excluding export
subsidies, received by the producer on export sales
of product ℓ ;

a_i the volume of domestically produced intermediate inputs of
type

i   consumed by the activity;

m_j the volume of imported intermediate inputs of type j;

p_i the basic price of intermediate input i, received by its
domestic producers;

p_j^m the c.i.f. price of the imported input j;

TT   all trade and transport margins on intermediate inputs between
the producer (or the border for imported inputs) and the buyer
(in this case the activity considered);

TC   all commodity taxes levied on intermediate inputs consumed by
the activity;

TN   all non-commodity taxes paid by the activity;

TI   all import taxes paid on imported inputs;

TE   all export taxes paid minus subsidies received on export
sales.

It should be observed that in formula (5.4) intermediate inputs are not
valued at buyers' prices - as they should be according to the definition
of value-added -, but at basic (or c.i.f.) prices. The difference
between the two valuations is accounted for by the separate terms TT, TC
and TI.

In formula (5.4) the valuation of intermediate inputs has been
chosen at basic prices because nominal rates of protection are
formulated in terms of basic prices. Thus basic prices are convenient
for the conversion of the valuation of intermediate inputs to free-trade
prices. Moreover there is a close connection with the way that

intermediate inputs, trade and transport margins and indirect taxes are
usually registered in input-output tables. The valuation of exports at
export-tax-inclusive (subsidy-exclusive) prices is chosen to facilitate
the transition to the input-output approach to be dealt with in section
5.3.

5.2.2 Value-Added at Free-Trade Prices

In the following subsections it is shown how the value-added that
would be obtained by the activity can be estimated with the production
of the same basket of goods, but under free-trade conditions. The
assumptions necessary to come to such an estimate are stated briefly.
But first, formula (5.4) is rewritten for the free-trade situation:

$$(5.5) \quad y^{ft} = \Sigma_k q_k p_k^{ft} + \Sigma_\ell e_\ell p_\ell^{e,ft} - \Sigma_i a_i^{ft} p_i^{ft} - \Sigma_j m_j^{ft} p_j^{m,ft}$$

$$-TM^{ft} - TC^{ft} - TN^{ft} - TI^{ft} - TE^{ft}$$

The superscript 'ft' relates the symbols to the free-trade situation.
Thus the value-added y^{ft} stands for the value-added that would be
obtained under free-trade conditions with the production of the
protection basket. This value-added is referred to as value-added at
free-trade prices.

It should be noted that the only symbols without superscripts are
the q's and the e's. This does not imply that the basket of goods
produced by the activity is assumed to remain unaffected by the
transition to the free-trade situation. Contrary to such an assumption,
both the level and the composition of production are allowed to change
in reality. But according to the definition of the effective rate, it is
the value-added generated with the production of the same basket that
interests us. It could be argued that shifts may occur within the same
basket from domestic to export sales: to avoid major complications of
minor importance, it is preferred to interpret the definition of the
effective rate in such a way that the baskets involved in domestic and
export sales are perfectly separated.

5.2.3 A Rigid Input Structure

The next step is to assume that the structure of intermediate

inputs does not change and that there is no substitution between
domestically produced and imported inputs:

$$(5.6a,b) \qquad a_i^{ft} = a_i \qquad and \qquad m_j^{ft} = m_j$$

Needless to say that as soon as information is available on how
intermediate inputs would respond to the elimination of the protective
system, there is nothing against adjusting the input structure to the
new situation; but as a rule such information is not even available for
an individual industry, let alone on an economy-wide basis.

There are some economy-wide studies[9] which attempt to simulate the
free-trade input structure with the aid of free-trade input-output coefficients. The coefficients are then estimated using the input-output
table of a country with a relatively non-interventionist policy in
respect of foreign trade. In these studies the coefficients of the
protection situation are not usually from reality but by applying the
nominal rates to the free-trade coefficients. As a consequence, there is
no accounting for substitution among inputs either and the only
difference is that effective protection is calculated on a different
input structure from the one observed.

If on the other hand the free-trade coefficients obtained as
described should be compared direct with the coefficients observed in
the protection situation, the resulting effective rates of protection
would mix up protection with international differences in input-output
coefficients and the results would become extremely unreliable.

5.2.4 Adjustment of Indirect Taxation to the Free-Trade Situation

Following the assumptions adopted in Chapter 2 regarding indirect
taxation, indirect domestic commodity and non-commodity taxes are
maintained under free trade while import and export taxes are abolished.
Assuming also a rigid input structure, this implies that the terms TC
and TN are not affected so that the corresponding superscripts 'ft' may
be suppressed ($TC^{ft}=TC$ and $TN^{ft}=TN$) and the foreign-trade tax terms
disappear ($TI^{ft}=0$ and $TE^{ft}=0$).

As explained earlier[10] it is possible that the mechanism of the

9. See, for example, Balassa et al. (1971), pp. 14-16.
10. See section 2.5.

indirect-tax system in the protection situation requires border tax
adjustments for the free-trade situation. This occurs, for example, if
domestic commodity taxes are not due on importation of equivalent
products. In such cases part of the import tariff is assumed to
substitute the domestic commodity tax and only the remaining part is
protective. By incorporating the substituting part of the import tariff
in the domestic-commodity-tax terms of formula (5.4), that sort of
complication is avoided from the start. Similarly it is recommended
treating domestic commodity taxes which are not paid back on exportation
as if they were export taxes.

5.2.5 Revaluation of Output

Hypothetical free-trade prices for the different components of
output are implicitly given in the nominal protective rates. In fact it
can easily be proved that:

$$(5.7) \qquad \Sigma_k q_k p_k^{ft} = \Sigma_k q_k \frac{p_k}{1 + w_k} = \frac{1}{1 + w_0} \Sigma_k q_k p_k$$

In other words the output for sales in the domestic market is
valued at free-trade prices by dividing the value at protection prices
($q_k p_k$) of each of the components by 1 plus the nominal protective rate
of that component or by dividing the real value of the whole basket by 1
plus the nominal rate of the basket.[11] . These rates can be ordinary or
net rates depending whether or not the exchange rate is adjusted.

As far as exports are concerned it is assumed that the export-tax-
inclusive prices p_ℓ^e are not affected by the transition to the free-trade
situation. Only if there is an exchange rate adjustment ϕ, the export
prices p_ℓ^e expressed in domestic currency must be multiplied by a factor
$(1 + \phi)$. As a result of these assumptions:

$$(5.8) \qquad p_\ell^{e,ft} = p_\ell^e (1 + \phi)$$

It should be noted from equation (5.8) that it is not concluded, except
for a currency devaluation, that the industry's net export receipts on

11. See subsection 3.5.1.

the exported basket would not be affected. Evidently the elimination of
the export tax or subsidy has a direct effect on those receipts, but
this effect is accounted for in the separate term TE.

5.2.6 Revaluation of Tradable Inputs

All imported inputs are tradable by definition. It is assumed that
their c.i.f. import prices in foreign-currency terms are not affected by
the transition to the free-trade situation and as their valuation in
equation (5.4) is at c.i.f. prices, this leads to:

$$(5.9) \qquad p_j^{m,ft} = p_j^m (1 + \phi)$$

Once more the gain on import taxes is accounted for separately by the
term TI.

Intermediate inputs from domestic origin should be divided into
tradable and non-tradable inputs. The treatment given to the non-
tradables is discussed in subsection 5.2.7. Revaluation of the tradable
inputs is performed in the same way as that of outputs, that is, by
dividing their protection value by 1 plus the applicable nominal
protective rate:

$$(5.10) \qquad \Sigma_i a_i p_i^{ft} = \Sigma_i a_i \frac{p_i}{1 + w_i} \qquad (i = \text{tradable})$$

where the summation is over tradable inputs only. Note that such a
revaluation can only be carried out if the intermediate-input structure
a_i is known at the same level of detail as nominal protection.

Only in exceptional cases, perhaps for a specific economic
activity, would such information be available at the product level, but
as a rule, particularly in economy-wide calculations of effective
protection, the input structure of the industries is given at a much
higher level of aggregation, usually coinciding with the level of sector
aggregation adopted in the input-output table.

In the absence of more detailed information about input structures,
there is no other way than to revalue the inputs group-wise. In
calculations with input-output tables, all inputs coming from a specific
sector are converted to free-trade valuation with the aid of the nominal
protective rate applying to the output of that sector as a whole. By

doing so, it is assumed that the nominal rate of the output of the
sector is uniformly applicable to all its constituent flows. This
assumption is referred to as the assumption of uniform revaluation of
input-output rows.

If the intra-sector composition of input flows varies notably from
sector to sector, the uniform revaluation of input-output rows may lead
to biases in the results. These biases tend to be stronger, the higher
the variation of nominal rates among the products constituting the
output. In principle it is possible to improve on the quality of
effective-protection estimates by allowing non-uniform revaluation of
input-output rows, but to that end more detailed information is
indispensable.

5.2.7 Revaluation of Non-Tradable Inputs

For non-tradable goods and services there is no way to measure
nominal rates of protection. Due to their non-tradability there are no
international quotations available, nor are they included in the tariff
lists. A way out would be to compare their prices with those holding in
other countries. But first, the prices holding in other countries may
also be affected by the protective systems there, and second, even if
this should not be the case, there is no reason to believe that under
free-trade conditions the prices in the country under study would become
equal to those in other countries.

For that reason it is necessary to make an assumption in respect of
the valuation of the non-tradable goods and services (including the
trade and transport margins of the term TT) under free-trade conditions.
In the following, four alternatives are distinguished:

a. The original Balassa method

In this method, the free-trade prices of the non-tradables are
assumed to be the same as those holding in the protection
situation. In other words, nominal protection of the non-tradables
is supposed to be zero.

b. The modified Balassa method

Here the assumption is that changes in intermediate-input costs
of the non-tradables are shifted to their prices. This implies
that the value-added generated with their production remains

unaffected by the transition to the free-trade situation. In other words it is assumed that effective protection to the sectors producing non-tradables is zero.

c. The original Scott method

According to this method the prices of the non-tradables follow the average trend of the tradables. That is, if on the average the tradables are 20 per cent cheaper under free trade, all non-tradable inputs would be deflated by a uniform percentage of 20 per cent. Thus it is assumed that nominal protection of the non-tradables is uniform and equal to the average nominal protection of the tradables. The weights that should be taken to form the average are discussed in Chapter 6.

d. The modified Scott method[12]

Here the value-added generated with the production of the non-tradables is assumed to follow the average trend of the value added generated by the sectors producing tradables. This is equivalent to assuming that there is a uniform effective protection to sectors producing non-tradables equal to the average effective protection given to sectors producing tradables.

All these methods, together with the so-called Corden method, which is not based on a specific revaluation device for the non-tradables, are elaborated in Chapter 6. In the numerical example, section 5.5, the present chapter, the original Balassa method is followed to avoid unnecessary complications in the exposition of the effective protective rate.

5.2.8 Premiums to Licenceholders and Trade Margins

If the inputs from abroad are imported direct by the consumer industry, the premium to the licenceholder accrues to that industry. If on the other hand imported inputs are led through the trade sector, the latter sector holds the licence and the premium is included in the term TT of formula (5.4).

Similar observations can be made regarding exported output. If the industry holds the licence for exportation the premium is included in

12. This method is a symmetrical extension of the original Scott method. It was suggested by Kuyvenhoven (1978), p. 170.

the prices p_ℓ^e received by the producer on export sales. But if exports
are led through the trade sector it is not included in these prices and
does not appear at all among the positive terms of equation (5.4).

These premiums must be removed from the corresponding trade margins
in the free-trade situation. Thus to come to a proper definition of the
term TT^{ft} of equation (5.5), first the premiums on indirectly imported
inputs should be deducted from TT and then the remaining part of the
trade margins should be revalued according to one of the methods set out
in subsection 5.2.7. Likewise if a licence is required for exportation,
premiums on indirectly exported output should be incorporated in the
free-trade export prices $p_\ell^{e,ft}$ and equation (5.8) should be adjusted
accordingly.

5.3   Input-Output Calculations of Effective Protection

5.3.1 Converting the Valuation of an Input-Output Table from Protection to Free-Trade Prices

For economy-wide calculations of effective protection an input-
output table for the economy under study is indispensable. In this
section it is shown how effective rates of protection can be calculated
by changing the existing valuation of such an input-output table to a
valuation at free-trade prices. This is performed by first revaluing all
flows of goods and services at free-trade prices, then adjusting the
indirect taxes to the free-trade conditions and finally obtaining the
value-added flows of the new table as residues in the columns. These
value-added flows correspond precisely with the concept of value added
at free-trade prices according to its definition (5.5). The effective
rates of protection can then be calculated by comparing the value-added
flows of the original with those of the new table.

Most theoretical introductions to effective protection[13] do not
express the effective rate in terms of input-output flows but rather
of coefficients. Although both approaches are essentially equivalent,
the conversion of flow tables to free-trade valuation is simpler and
gives a better insight into what is really at stake. Moreover in a

---

13. All standard descriptions of the effective protective rate use coef-
     ficients. See, for example, Corden (1971), pp. 35-40.

formulation in terms of flows the economy-wide balancing of nominal and effective protection, which is dealt with in section 5.4 and further elaborated in Chapter 8, becomes immediately clear.

5.3.2 The Existing Input-Output Table

Most input-output tables are valued at producers' prices, that is, flows of goods and services include indirect commodity taxes but are net of trade and transport margins. As a consequence the row of indirect taxes registers commodity taxes according to the producing (not the consuming) industry.[14] However as nominal protective rates are defined in terms of commodity-tax-exclusive basic prices, it is convenient to convert such input-output tables first to a valuation at basic prices. In the latter form of valuation the tax row registers taxes according to the consuming sector.

If the input-output table serves as the starting point for effective-protection calculations, it is preferable to make an exception for export flows. In order not to lose sight of the formulas used in section 5.2, these flows should be valued at their export-tax-inclusive (subsidy-exclusive) prices so that the net-indirect-tax row includes, apart from net taxes on inputs, net export taxes on exported output.

Another complication may derive from the registration of import taxes. Even in tables valued at producers' prices - that is, flows are tax-inclusive-imports are usually valued at c.i.f. prices, that is, excluding import taxes. These latter taxes are then considered to form part of the trade margins so they are included in the trade row. At the same time they are accounted for as indirect taxes in the column of the trade sector. Consequently the entry at the intersection of the indirect-tax row with the trade column includes the import taxes paid on the complete import bill of the country.

For the purpose of effective-protection calculations it is preferable to separate these import taxes from the trade margins and register them in the indirect-tax row according to their economic destination.

As a consequence of the proposed form of registration, the net-

---

14. For a description of different forms of registration and valuation in input-output tables, see United Nations (1973), ch. 3; or Bulmer-Thomas (1982), ch. 6 and 7.

indirect-tax row contains the following three elements:

i.   net indirect commodity taxes on inputs plus non-commodity taxes?

ii.   net import taxes on imported inputs;

iii. net export taxes on exported output.

In view of the differential treatment of these taxes under free-trade valuation, it is preferable to keep these three components separate. In the numerical example (section 5.5) the conversion from the usual registration of taxes to the one advocated is demonstrated.

In this way the following input-output table is obtained, which serves as the starting point for the conversion to free-trade valuation:

Table 5.1 Input-Output Table at Basic Prices in the Protection Situation

Sectors	Tradables	Non-Tradables	Exports	Domestic Fin.Dem.	Total
Tradables	A_{TT}	A_{TN}	E_T	DFD_T	X_T
Non-tradables	A_{NT}	A_{NN}	E_N	DFD_N	X_N
Imports	M_T	M_N	–	M_F	M_{TOT}
Net Ind. Taxes	IT_T	IT_N	–	IT_F	IT_{TOT}
a. domestic	(TD_T)	(TD_N)	(–)	(TD_F)	(TD_{TOT})
b. import	(TI_T)	(TI_N)	(–)	(TI_F)	(TI_{TOT})
c. export	(TE_T)	(TE_N)	(–)	(–)	$(TE_{TOT}$
Value Added	Y_T	Y_N	–	Y_{GOV}	Y_{TOT}
Total X_T	X_N	E_{TOT}	DFD_{TOT}		

where A   stands for intermediate deliveries
      E   for exports
      DFD for domestic final demand
      X   for value of production
      M   for imports
      IT   for net indirect taxes
      TD   for net indirect domestic taxes, i.e. commodity plus non-
           commodity
      TI   for net import taxes
      TE   for net export taxes
      Y   for value-added ($Y = X - \iota A - M - IT$)

and subscripts

T   refers to sectors producing tradables

N   sectors producing non-tradables

E   exports

F   domestic final demand

GOV government

TOT total

The sectors have been ordered in such a way that all those producing tradables come before those producing non-tradables. Note that there are no tax entries in the export column. As export taxes (net of subsidies) are registered with the producing sector, the row is empty in the fourth quadrant. Also, domestic indirect taxes applicable to exports are registered under the producing sector. If these taxes should be normal commodity taxes, the border tax adjustment would incorporate them in the export taxes. If there are taxes on depletable natural resources, they should be treated as if they were non-commodity taxes. The rows of domestic, import and export taxes have been placed within parentheses to indicate that they should not be taken into account in the summation of the columns. They merely represent a decomposition of the net-indirect-tax row (IT = TD + TI + TE).

The trade sector is considered among the sectors producing non-tradable services. In principle trading services can be imported and exported but as a rule domestic trading is carried out by national companies. Exports of the trade sector mainly comprise domestic margins on exported goods but may also contain margins earned abroad by national companies. In spite of the fact that these and also some other services are exported (expressed by the contradictory term E_N, exports of non-tradables), the goods and services produced by those sectors for the domestic market are supposed to be non-tradable.

Finally it should be observed that trade and transport margins are registered according to the so-called producers' point of view. This means that the margins appearing in the rows for trade and transport are classified according to their economic destination and that flows are valued at prices excluding the margins between producer and consumer. As nominal rates of protection are formulated in terms of basic prices, the exclusion of the margins from the flows provides a proper starting point for the revaluation procedure.

5.3.3 Revaluation of the Input-Output Table at Free-Trade Prices

For simplicity's sake it is assumed from now on that there is no adjustment of the exchange rate to the free-trade situation. In Chapter 7 where the exchange rate adjustment is discussed in detail, this assumption is relaxed. Generally the revaluation procedure can be divided into six consecutive steps:

Step 1. Revaluation of Tradable Flows

The tradable flows A_{TT}, A_{TN} and DFD_T are revalued by dividing each of them by one plus the nominal protective rate of the corresponding row. By dividing all flows of a row uniformly by one single factor, it is precisely here that the assumption of uniform revaluation enters. Denoting the diagonal matrix of nominal protective rates by $\hat{W}_T$, the revaluation can be expressed as follows:

$$(5.11a) \qquad A_{TT}^{ft} = (I + \hat{W}_T)^{-1} A_{TT} = \hat{V}_T A_{TT}$$

$$(5.11b) \qquad A_{TN}^{ft} = (I + \hat{W}_T)^{-1} A_{TN} = \hat{V}_T A_{TN}$$

$$(5.11c) \qquad DFD_T^{ft} = (I + \hat{W}_T)^{-1} DFD_T = \hat{V}_T DFD_T$$

where $\hat{V}_T$ is the diagonal matrix of row deflators. Exports are not revalued in the same way. As they were valued at tax-inclusive export prices they are supposed to remain unaffected. Should there be indirect exportation subject to licensing, then the premiums to the licenceholders would have to be moved from the exports of the trade sector to those of the producing sector, but for simplicity this is excluded by assumption.

$$(5.11d) \qquad E_T^{ft} = E_T$$

Finally the sums of the rows X_T^{ft} are adjusted by summing up the new flows valued at free-trade prices:

$$(5.11e) \quad X_T^{ft} = (I + \hat{W}_T)^{-1} (X_T - E_T) + E_T = \hat{V}_T (X_T - E_T) + E_T$$

Step 2. <u>Revaluation of Non-Tradable Flows</u>

The revaluation of the non-tradable flows A_{NT}, A_{NN} and DFD_N is essentially the same as that of their tradable counterparts. The only difference is that for the non-tradeable goods and services the nominal rates of protection are not estimated in the way described in Chapter 4, but defined by one of the assumptions mentioned in subsection 5.2.7. Denoting the diagonal matrices of the resulting nominal rates by $\hat{W}_N$ and the corresponding deflation indices by $\hat{V}_N$, the conversion can be written as follows:

$$(5.12a) \quad A_{NT}^{ft} = (I + \hat{W}_N)^{-1} A_{NT} = \hat{V}_N A_{NT}$$

$$(5.12b) \quad A_{NN}^{ft} = (I + \hat{W}_N)^{-1} A_{NN} = \hat{V}_N A_{NN}$$

$$(5.12c) \quad DFD_N^{ft} = (I + \hat{W}_N)^{-1} DFD_N = \hat{V}_N DFD_N$$

$$(5.12d) \quad E_N^{ft} = E_N$$

And again the rows are totalled:

$$(5.12e) \quad X_N^{ft} = (I + \hat{W}_N)^{-1} (X_N - E_N) + E_N = \hat{V}_N (X_N - E_N) + E_N$$

Finally if there is indirect importation subject to licensing, the premiums to licenceholders should be deducted from the flows appearing in the trade row before the row is deflated. In order not to complicate the notation it is assumed that there is no indirect importation, but in case there is the according changes can be carried out in a straightforward manner.

Step 3. <u>Revaluation of imports</u>

In the input-output table imports are valued at c.i.f. prices. Thus a revaluation at free-trade prices does not make them change:

(5.13) $M_J^{ft} = M_J$ (J = T,N,F,TOT)

Step 4. Adjustment of Indirect Taxes

The adjustment of indirect taxes to the free-trade situation is been set out in subsection 5.2.3. Generally the domestic taxes are not affected:

(5.14a) $TD_J^{ft} = TD_J$ (J = T,N,E,F,TOT),

while the import and export taxes disappear:

(5.14b) $TI_J^{ft} = 0$ (J = T,N,F,TOT)

(5.14c) $TE_J^{ft} = 0$ (J = T,N,TOT)

It is assumed that border tax adjustments, whenever necessary, have already been carried out in the protection situation.

Step 5. Transfer of the Values of Production

The next step is to make the column sums over the first and third quadrants equal to the row sums over the first and second quadrants, the latter representing the production of the productive sectors valued at free-trade prices.

Step 6. Value Added Adjustment

The value-added of the productive sectors at free-trade prices Y_T^{ft} or Y_N^{ft} can now be defined as a residue that makes the corresponding column fit its prescribed total X_T^{ft} or X_N^{ft}.

(5.15a) $Y_T^{ft} = V_T(\hat{X}_T - \hat{E}_T - A_{TT}) - V_N A_{NT} + E_T - M_T - TD_T$

(5.15b) $Y_N^{ft} = V_N(\hat{X}_N - \hat{E}_N - A_{NN}) - V_T A_{TN} + E_N - M_N - TD_N$

where V_T and V_N are row vectors of row deflators. It is worth noting that formulas (5.15a, b) are straightforward interpretations of the definition of value-added at free-trade prices expressed by equation (5.5). Finally the value-added generated by the government is assumed to remain unchanged with the transition to the free-trade situation.

(5.15c) $Y_{GOV}^{ft} = Y_{GOV}$

This assumption is somewhat arbitrary, but it is only made to complete the table at free-trade prices and by no means interferes in the definition of the effective rates of the productive sectors. In order to close the procedure, the value added row and the final demand columns are totalled.

5.3.4 The Input-Output Table at Free-Trade Prices

As a result of the consecutive steps of revaluation in subsection 5.3.3, the following input-output table is obtained:

Table 5.2   Input-Output Table: at free-trade prices

Sectors	Tradables	Non-Tradables	Exports	Domestic Fin.Dem.	Total
Tradables	$\hat{V}_T A_{TT}$	$\hat{V}_T A_{TN}$	E_T	$\hat{V}_T DFD_T$	X_T^{ft}
Non-tradables	$\hat{V}_N A_{NT}$	$\hat{V}_N A_{NN}$	E_N	$\hat{V}_N DFD_N$	X_N^{ft}
Imports	M_T	M_N	M_F	M_{TOT}	
Net Ind.Taxes	IT_T^{ft}	IT_N^{ft}	$-$	IT_F^{ft}	IT_{TOT}^{ft}
a. domestic	(TD_T)	(TD_N)	$-$	(TD_F)	(TD_{TOT})
b. import	$(-)$	$(-)$	$(-)$	$(-)$	$(-)$
c. export	$(-)$	$(-)$	$(-)$	$(-)$	$(-)$
Value-Added	Y_T^{ft}	Y_N^{ft}	$-$	Y_{GOV}	Y_{TOT}^{ft}
Total	X_T^{ft}	X_N^{ft}	E_{TOT}	DFD_{TOT}^{ft}	$-$

The table is organised in the same way as protection prices (Table 5.1). Note that the rows corresponding to foreign-trade taxes are empty so that the net-indirect-tax row becomes equal to the domestic constituent row. As the value-added of the productive sectors is defined as a residue, it may result negative. Although this case is not common, it occurs whenever total intermediate inputs of a sector valued at tax-inclusive free-trade prices exceeds the tax-exclusive free-trade value of its output.

5.3.5 Effective Protection in Absolute Terms and its Decomposition

The effective rate of protection is defined in relative terms by measuring the difference between value-added at protection and at free-trade prices relative to the value-added at free-trade prices. However effective protection can also be measured in absolute terms by just taking the difference between the two concepts:

(5.16a) $\quad G_T = Y_T - Y_T^{ft}$

(5.16b) $\quad G_N = Y_N - Y_N^{ft}$

By introducing the expressions (5.15) into (5.16), effective protection in absolute terms can be written as:

(5.17a) $\quad G_T = (\iota_T - V_T)(\hat{X}_T - \hat{E}_T - A_{TT}) - (\iota_N - V_N) A_{NT} - (TI_T + TE_T)$

(5.17b) $\quad G_N = (\iota_N - V_N)(\hat{X}_N - \hat{E}_N - A_{NN}) - (\iota_T - V_T) A_{TN} - (TI_N + TE_N)$

Equations (5.17) decompose effective protection in two elements: protection derived from output (i) and protection derived from inputs (ii).

By subtracting the input-output table at free-trade prices (Table 5.2) from that at protection prices (Table 5.1), a new table is obtained in which all terms appearing in equations (5.17) are contained:

Table 5.3 Decomposition of Effective Protection

Protection	Tradables	Non-Tradables	Ex-ports	Domestic Fin.Dem.	Total
1. Output	$(I-V_T)(X_T-E_T)$	$(I-V_N)(X_N-E_N)$		$DFD_{TOT}-DFD_{TOT}^{ft}$	-
2. Inputs: (a)+(b)+(c)+(d)					
a. Tradables	$(I-\hat{V}_T)A_{TT}$	$(I-\hat{V}_T)A_{TN}$	-	$(I-\hat{V}_T)DFD_T$	$(I-\hat{V}_T)(X_T-E_T)$
b. Non-Trad.	$(I-\hat{V}_N)A_{NT}$	$(I-\hat{V}_N)A_{NN}$	-	$(I-\hat{V}_N)DFD_N$	$(I-\hat{V}_N)(X_N-E_N)$
c. Imports	-	-	-	-	-
d. Ind.Taxes	$TI_T + TE_T$	$TI_N + TE_N$	-	TI_F	$TI_{TOT} + TE_{TOT}$
3. Effective (1)-(2) Protection:	G_T	G_N	-	-	-

By a rearrangement of the rows of the difference table, the
decomposition of effective protection is made explicit. Protection of
output, which corresponds to the difference between the column totals of
Tables 5.1 and 5.2, is put in the first row. Then protection of inputs
is split up according to the sector classification of the input-output
table. Effective protection is obtained by subtracting protection of
inputs from that of output.

    From a policy point of view such difference tables are interesting.
They allow the policy maker to trace, to a certain extent, the sources
of effective protection. For example, the direct impact of a pricing
policy for fuels (supported by protective measures) upon the value-
added of the different sectors of the economy can be read immediately
from the corresponding rows of such tables. Indirect effects -
electricity prices are also affected - are not directly visible. They
are somehow included in the non-tradable input part of the table. How
such indirect effects through the non-tradables can be brought back to
the tradable prime cause is explained in Chapter 6.

5.4   Implications

5.4.1 National Accounting Identities

By conceiving protection as the result of a revaluation of an input-output table at free-trade prices, several properties become evident which in a coefficient approach would remain under the surface. For example, due to the fact that row sums equal column sums for the productive sectors, it follows immediately that the sum of the flows of the second quadrant is equal to the sum of the flows of the third. Adding the sum of the fourth quadrant on both sides arrives at the well-known national accounting identity which states that gross domestic product (value-added at factor costs plus net indirect taxes) plus imports equals domestic final demand (final consumption and investments) plus exports. The validity of this identity does not depend on the specific type of valuation. It holds equally well with protection as with free-trade prices. That is:

$$(5.18a) \qquad Y_{TOT} + IT_{TOT} + M_{TOT} = DFD_{TOT} + E_{TOT}$$

$$(5.18b) \qquad Y_{TOT}^{ft} + IT_{TOT}^{ft} + M_{TOT} = DFD_{TOT}^{ft} + E_{TOT}$$

By substracting identity (5.18b) from (5.18a), the following expression for the total effective protection in absolute terms is found:

$$(5.19) \qquad G_{TOT} = Y_{TOT} - Y_{TOT}^{ft} = (DFD_{TOT} - DFD_{TOT}^{ft}) - (TI_{TOT} + TE_{TOT})$$

Reading the indirect-tax terms on the left-hand side, equation (5.19) ex-presses that total effective protection to the productive sectors G_{TOT} plus effective protection to the government in the form of foreign-trade taxes ($TI_{TOT} + TE_{TOT}$) equals total nominal protection on the domestic-final-demand basket. In other words the gains from protection accruing to the productive sectors and the government is lost in the deterioration of purchasing power.

5.4.2 Averaging Nominal and Effective Protection

With the aid of the definition of effective protection in relative terms (5.1) and in absolute terms (5.16), total protection G^{TOT} can be written as:

$$(5.20) \qquad G_{TOT} = (Y_T - Y_T^{ft}) \iota_T + (Y_N - Y_N^{ft}) \iota_N = Y_T^{ft} Z_T + Y_N^{ft} Z_N$$

where ι_T and ι_N are column vectors of units for the summation of the row
vectors Y_T, Y_T^{ft}, Y_N and Y_N^{ft}, respectively; and

Z_T and Z_N are column vectors of effective rates of protection
for sectors producing tradables (Z_T) and non-tradables
(Z_N).

In this way the left-hand side of equation (5.19) is written as a
weighted sum of the effective rates.

Similarly the terms $(DFD_{TOT} - DFD_{TOT}^{ft})$ which appear on the right-
hand side can be expressed as a weighted sum of the nominal rates of
protection:

$$(5.21) \qquad DFD_{TOT} - DFD_{TOT}^{ft} = \iota_T (DFD_T - DFD_T^{ft}) + \iota_N (DFD_N - DFD_N^{ft}) + TI_F$$

$$= W_T DFD_T^{ft} + W_N DFD_N^{ft} + W_M M_F$$

where ι_T and ι_N are now conceived as row vectors of units to sum up
column vectors of domestic final demand;

W_T and W_N are row vectors of nominal rates of protection by
sector, the latter being defined by the assumption
concerning the non-tradables;

W_M is the nominal protective rate applicable to imports
for domestic final demand, defined as TI_F/M_F.

The remaining terms on the right-hand side of equation (5.19)
represent tax revenues from foreign-trade taxes. When they are
transferred to the left-hand side so that there is a change of sign,
they can be interpreted as protection to the government. Defining an
effective rate of protection to the indirect-tax system as:

$$(5.22) \qquad Z_{IT} = (TI_{TOT} + TE_{TOT})/TD_{TOT}$$

and substituting expressions (5.20, 21 and 22) into (5.19) the following identity is obtained:

$$(5.23) \qquad Y_T^{ft} Z_T + Y_N^{ft} Z_N + TD_{TOT} Z_{IT} = W_T DFD_T^{ft} + W_N DFD_N^{ft} + W_M M_F$$

The left-hand side of identity (5.23) looks like the numerator of a weighted average of effective rates and the right-hand side like one of nominal rates. However the denominator required on the left-hand side ($Y_{TOT}^{ft} - Y_{GOV} + TD_{TOT}$) is not the same as the denominator which is required on the right-hand side ($DFD_{TOT}^{ft} - Y_{GOV}$). According to identity (5.18b) the difference consists of the balance of payments deficit ($M_{TOT} - E_{TOT}$).

But it is possible to interpret identity (5.23) as an equivalence of average nominal and average effective protection. To that end both sides of the identity should be divided by ($DFD_{TOT}^{ft} - Y_{GOV}$) so that the right-hand side expresses a proper weighted average of nominal rates. By imagining an extra term on the left-hand side equal to the deficit ($M_{TOT} - E_{TOT}$) multiplied by an effective rate of protection to the foreign-exchange system equal to zero, the left-hand side also becomes a proper weighted average, now of effective protection.

The effective rate of protection of the foreign-exchange system is zero as a result of the absence of an exchange rate adjustment. In Chapter 8 however it is demonstrated that, if the exchange rate is adjusted to the free-trade situation, the effective protective rate of the foreign exchange system no longer disappears and can be shown to have a significant interpretation.

A similar equivalence between average nominal and average effective protection was found by Leith.[15] However he states the equivalence using value-added at market prices (including indirect taxes) as weights for the effective rates and final demand (including exports) minus imports as weights for the nominal rates.

15. See Leith (1971).

5.5   Numerical Example

5.5.1 The Input-Output Table at Producers' Prices
To highlight the most important elements of the preceding discussion, a numerical example is presented. The point of departure is the
following input-output table in which four sectors are distinguished:

1. primary - consisting of agriculture and mining
2. industry - comprising the manufacturing industries
3. trade - consisting of trade and transport
4. others - that is, construction, electricity and the remaining
   services, including the government.

It is assumed that all commodities produced by the first two
sectors are tradable while goods and services produced by the latter two
are supposed to be non-tradable. Imports are registered in a non-
competitive way, that is, as a row in the third and fourth quadrants
according to sectors of destination.

Table 5.4   Input-Output Table: at producers' prices
            (in millions of pesos)

Sectors	1	2	3	4	Sub-total	Ex-ports	Domest. Fin.Dem.	Total
1. Primary	282	655	-	93	1030	413	1293	2736
2. Industry	244	515	104	280	1143	333	1025	2501
3. Trade	147	199	146	157	649	108	844	1601
tax on imp.)	(26)	(35)	(10)	(14)	(85)	(-)	(120)	(205)
4. Others	115	128	244	320	807	-	2050	2857
Subtotal	788	1497	494	850	3629	854	5212	9695
5. Imports	133	212	54	61	460	-	751	1211
6. Ind.Taxes	84	65	286	41	476	-	-	476
(imp.taxes)	-	-	(169)	-	(169)	-	-	(169)
(exp.taxes)	(20)	(-15)	-	-	(5)	-	-	(5)
(com.taxes)	(47)	(60)	(112)	(26)	(245)	-	-	(245)
(n.c.taxes)	(17)	(20)	(5)	(15)	(57)	-	-	(57)
7. Value-Added	1731	727	767	1905	5130	-	-	5130
Total	2736	2501	1601	2857	9695	854	5963	-

As in most input-output tables, valuation is at producers' prices, that is, trade and transport margins are not included in the flows, but indirect commodity taxes are. Trade and transport margins are accounted for in a separate row as a common cost factor on the inputs of the buying sector. Exports of the trade sector comprise domestic trade and transport margins on exported goods plus margins earned abroad by national trading and transport companies.

5.5.2 Registration of Indirect Taxes Net of Subsidies

The incidence of indirect taxation upon each of the sectors of the economy by the type of taxes is given in Table 5.5. It should be noted that the commodity taxes registered in the first part of this table are included in the corresponding flows of the input-output Table 5.4. To give an example, the 7 million pesos paid on inputs from the primary sectors into industry form part of the 655 million entry in the input-output table.

Table 5.5 <u>Net Indirect Taxes</u> (in millions of pesos)

Sectors	1	2	3	4	Sub-total	Domestic Fin.Dem.	Total
Domestic Commodity Taxes on Inputs	14	38	17	15	84	161	245
from: 1. Primary	3	7	-	2	12	35	47
2. Industry	3	6	4	4	17	43	60
3. Trade	4	17	5	4	30	46	76
4. Others	-	1	2	1	4	22	26
5. Imports	4	7	6	4	21	15	36
Other Taxes	59	33	9	25	126	105	231
6. Import Taxes	22	28	4	10	64	105	169
7. Export Taxes	20	-15	-	-	5	-	5
8. Non-Commod.	17	20	5	15	57	-	57
Total Taxes	73	71	26	40	210	266	476

Imports in Table 5.4 are valued at c.i.f. prices, that is, import taxes and domestic commodity taxes on imports are not included. Instead they are led through the trade sector and afterwards compensated in the flow of 286 million at the intersection of the indirect-tax row with the trade column. In the input-output table these taxes on imports are explicitly mentioned below the trade row, but the figures are placed within parentheses to indicate that they already form part of the flows of the trade row. Thus imports of intermediate inputs for industry amounted to 212 million pesos at c.i.f. prices. Import taxes on these inputs were 28 million and domestic commodity taxes 7 million. Taken together, these taxes (35 million) form part of the flow of 199 million which represent margins on intermediate inputs to industry.

Export taxes are included in the corresponding export flows, subsidies are excluded. Thus, the 413 million of primary product exports

includes 20 million of export taxes, but the net export subsidy of 15
million on manufactured exports does not form part of the corresponding
entry of 333 million.

The row of commodity taxes of the input-output Table 5.4 stands for
taxes on the output of the corresponding sectors. The first entry of 47
million, for example, coincides with the sum of the first row of the
indirect-tax Table 5.5. The entry of 112 million in the trade column is
obtained by combining total commodity taxes on imports (36 million) with
the sum of the third row (76 million).

5.5.3 Valuation of the Input-Output Table: at basic prices

In order to arrive at a valuation at basic prices the commodity
taxes must be excluded from the flows. In this way the following table
is obtained:

Table 5.6   Input-Output Table: at basic prices (in millions of pesos)

Sectors	1	2	3	4	Sub-total	Ex-ports	Dom. Fin.Dem.	Total
1. Primary	279	648	-	91	1018	413	1258	2689
2. Industry	241	509	100	276	1126	333	982	2441
3. Trade	117	147	131	139	534	108	678	1320
4. Others	115	127	242	319	803	-	2028	2831
Subtotal	752	1431	473	825	3481	854	4946	9281
5. Imports	133	212	54	61	460	-	751	1211
6. Ind.Taxes	73	71	26	40	210	-	266	476
(mp.taxes)	(22)	(28)	(4)	(10)	(64)	-	(105)	(169)
(exp.taxes)	(20)	(-15)	-	-	(5)	-	-	(5)
(com.taxes)	(14)	(38)	(17)	(15)	(84)	-	(161)	(247)
(n.c.taxes)	(17)	(20)	(5)	(15)	(57)	-	-	(57)
7. Value-Added	1731	727	767	1905	5130	-	-	5130
Total	2689	2441	1320	2831	9281	854	5963	-

Note that the value of inputs from the primary sector to industry
is reduced from 655 to 648 million and that of trade and transport
margins on inputs to industry from 199 first to 164 (excluding taxes on

imports) and then to 147 million (excluding commodity taxes on trade).
To make the table consistent, import taxes are no longer led through
trade but registered direct with the sector of destination. Moreover the
commodity tax row no longer represents taxes on the output of the
corresponding sector but on its inputs. It coincides with the column
totals of the commodity tax part of Table 5.5.

It should be noted that export taxes remain incorporated in the
export flows. This is not in accordance with a proper valuation at basic
prices but has been done to simplify the subsequent transition to a
valuation at free-trade prices.

5.5.4 Taxes and Prices under Free Trade

In the free-trade situation both import and export taxes and
subsidies are suppressed. However out of the 20 million export taxes on
primary commodities, 10 million substitute a domestic exploitation tax
on mineral resources which is not levied if the product is exported. As
these latter taxes are supposed to remain in force in the free-trade
situation, only 10 million out of the 20 million are suppressed, the
remaining 10 million being transferred to the non-commodity tax row. All
domestic components of indirect taxation (also commodity taxes on
imports) are supposed to remain intact in the free-trade situation.

The nominal rate of protection of the goods produced by the primary
sector is -2 per cent. In other words existing basic prices are 2 per
cent below free-trade prices. Nominal protection on manufactured goods
is 25 per cent. Thus the prices of manufactured goods are on average 25
per cent above the corresponding free-trade prices. Furthermore nominal
protection is supposed to be uniformly applicable to all flows contained
in a row of the input-output table excepting exports. In respect of the
non-tradable goods and services the assumption characteristic of the
original Balassa method is adopted, that is, free-trade prices are
assumed to be equal to protection prices.

5.5.5 Revaluation of the Input-Output Table

In order to arrive at a valuation at free-trade prices, the
following operations are carried out. The starting point is the table at
basic prices.

Row 1 The individual flows of the first row are divided by a factor
equal to 0.98, being 1 plus the nominal rate of protection of primary
goods. Only the export flow remains at its original level. The new row
sum is obtained by addition.

Row 2 A similar treatment is given to row 2 with the only
difference that now the dividing factor is 1.25.

Row 3 and 4 According to the assumption in respect of the prices of
the non-tradable goods and services, these rows remain unchanged.

Row 5 So does the row of imports, which remain valued at c.i.f.
prices.

Row 6 The net-indirect-tax row in the new table is equal to the sum
of the commodity and non-commodity components of the table at basic
prices. Note the transfer of 10 million from the export tax row to the
non-commodity tax row.

Row 7 The totals of the first four columns are equal to the newly
obtained sums of the corresponding rows. Then value-added by sector is
obtained as a residue between the new column totals and all other
entries of the column concerned.

(Sub)totals The remaining (sub)totals are defined by summation.

In this way, the following table is obtained:

Table 5.7 Input-Output Table: at free-trade prices
        (according to the original Balassa method)

Sectors	1	2	3	4	Sub-total	Ex-ports	Domestic Fin.Dem.	Total
1. Primary	285	661	-	93	1039	413	1284	2736
2. Industry	193	407	80	221	901	333	786	2020
3. Trade	117	147	131	139	534	108	678	1320
4. Others	115	127	242	319	803	-	2028	2831
Subtotal	710	1342	453	772	3277	854	4776	8907
5. Imports	133	212	54	61	460	-	751	1211
6. Ind.Taxes	41	58	22	30	151	-	161	312
7. Value Added	1852	408	791	1968	5019	-	-	5018
Total	2736	2020	1320	2831	8907	854	5688	-

5.5.6 Effective Protection and its Decomposition

Comparing the value-added row of Table 5.7 with that of Table 5.6, the following effective rates of protection are found:

Table 5.8 Effective Protection (in millions of pesos)

Sectors	Value-Added at under protection	Factor Costs under free trade	Effective Protection: Absolute	Effective Protection Relative%
1. Primary	1731	1852	- 121	- 6.5
2. Industry	727	408	319	78.2
3. Trade	767	791	- 24	- 3.0
4. Others	1905	1968	- 63	- 3.2
Total	5130	5019	111	2.2

Generally the protection spectrum in terms of effective rates is wider than that of nominal rates. Positive protection becomes more positive and negative protection more negative. As is to be expected, sectors producing non-tradables receive a slightly negative protection due to the, on average, positive protection on their inputs and the zero protection on their output under the present assumption.

The decomposition of effective protection in absolute terms is given in Table 5.9. The effective protection of the primary sector is minus 121 million, of which 47 million is derived from a negative protection on output, 42 million from positive protection on inputs and, finally, 32 million from foreign-trade taxes. The effective protection of industry is 319 million. If it were only for the output it would have been even higher (421), but 89 million is lost again on intermediate inputs and another 13 million on net foreign-trade taxes. As a result of the assumption of the original Balassa method, there are no entries for the intermediate inputs or outputs of non-tradables. For that reason the negative effective protection of the sectors producing non-tradables is exclusively derived from the higher input cost.

Table 5.9 Decomposition of Effective Protection
           (according to the original Balassa method)

Source	1	2	3	4	Sub-total	Ex-ports	Domestic Fin.Dem.	Total
a. Output	-47	421	-	-	374	-	275	649
b. Inputs:	74	102	24	63	263	-	275	538
1.Primary	(-6)	(-13)	(-)	(-2)	(-21)	(-)	(-26)	(-47)
2.Industry	(48)	(102)	(20)	(55)	(225)	(-)	(196)	(421)
3.Trade	(-)	(-)	(-)	(-)	(-)	(-)	(-)	(-)
4.Others	(-)	(-)	(-)	(-)	(-)	(-)	(-)	(-)
5.Imports	(-)	(-)	(-)	(-)	(-)	(-)	(-)	(-)
6.Ind.Taxes	(32)	(13)	(4)	(10)	(59)	(-)	(105)	(164)
c.Effective Protection:								
(a) - (b)	-121	319	-24	-63	111	-	-	111

As far as the national accounting identities are concerned, nominal protection in absolute terms on domestic final demand amounts to 170 million (4946 - 4776) on goods produced domestically and 105 million on imported items. Effective protection, on the other hand, equals 111 million (5130 - 5019) for the productive sectors and 164 million of extra tax collection for the government. Thus total nominal protection balances with total effective protection according to equations (5.19 and 5.23).

6 Non-tradable goods and services

6.1 Introductory Remarks

6.1.1 Non-Tradability

Goods or services are said to be <u>non-tradable</u> if they cannot possibly be traded internationally as a result of characteristics inherent in the goods or services themselves. The most common characteristics causing non-tradability of goods are: lack of mobility and perishability. For example, buildings cannot be traded among countries because they are not mobile and for reasons of perishability there is hardly any international trade in unprocessed cow's milk. It is also possible that a combination of these two factors makes a good non-tradable. Daily newspapers, for example, are almost always printed in the country itself even though present-day telecommunication facilities would permit editing and printing in another country as well.The high perishability of the news value together with high transportation costs by air make the goods practically non-tradable. There is definitely some international trade in newspapers, but here it mainly concerns a marginal market for tourists and foreign residents to whom it is less important what time the news arrives.

The latter example makes clear that it is not always easy to draw a clear line between tradability and non-tradability. Goods, though perfectly mobile, may be so little value-intensive that transport costs render them virtually non-tradable. Sand for construction purposes may serve as an example. But it may happen that a country is simply forced to ignore high transportation costs and import sand owing to a local shortage. Generally the tradability of goods becomes suspicious as soon as the price per metric ton fall below US 40 dollars (of 1980).

Contrary to goods, services are non-tradable as a rule. Many services, for example haircutting and restaurants, are produced at the place where they are consumed, which makes their tradability inconceivable. But there are also some services which can also be provided by firms from abroad, such as insurance, trade and transport. Nevertheless for effective-protection calculations they are usually treated as if they were non-tradable.

It should be mentioned that non-tradability is not the same thing as non-tradedness. There are other factors than non-tradability which may cause a product to be non-traded. Non-tradedness may be due to import restrictions, export impediments or to the simple fact that the domestic price happens to be between potential export and import prices, which makes international trade unprofitable even though the product in itself may be perfectly tradable. In this study non-tradability is clearly distinguished from non-tradedness. The latter term is often used in the literature on protection when in reality non-tradability is meant.

6.1.2 Free-Trade Prices for Non-Tradables

For tradable goods and services free-trade prices can be estimated from international prices as described in Chapter 3. For non-tradable goods and services international prices do not exist and the prices they would assume in the free-trade situation depend on domestic rather than international market conditions.

For example, as the output levels of highly protected industries tend to become smaller in the free-trade situation, their main non-tradable inputs are likely to become cheaper as a result of declining demand. The extent to which the prices of these inputs would decrease depends on a number of interrelated factors some of which are difficult to quantify. First, on the decline of intermediate demand: but if the product is also used for final purposes the price and income elasticities of final demand also play a role. And so does total income under free trade. Last but not least the supply elasticity of the goods should be mentioned, which in turn can be conceived as the combined effect of a production function and the conditions on the factor markets. The quantification of the above-mentioned factors is far from easy. It can only be done in the framework of a general-equilibrium model in the Walrasian sense.

6.1.3 General-Equilibrium Approach

The meaning of the term 'general-equilibrium model' is not unique.

Some authors[1] apply it to input-output models with endogenous final demand categories even when there is no price dependency in the demand system. It is also applied to Keynesian models referring to equilibrium in financial markets.[2] In the interpretation adopted here a proper general-equilibrium model is an economy-wide model in the Walrasian sense, that is, there is substitution and thus price dependency in the demand system and/or the production functions.[3]

The information requirements of such models are very high. Knowledge of production and consumption functions for all goods and services is indispensable. This does not only imply knowledge of actual supply and demand in existing circumstances, but also of hypothetical supply and demand in differing curcumstances. If it is possible to estimate such behaviour functions at all, the reliability of the information is doubtful as a rule.

Another problem is the manageability of general-equilibrium models. Usually their computation is incomparably more complicated than for their linear counterparts of the input-output type. For that reason problems of measurability and manageability are often solved in one stroke, by means of heroic assumptions that mould a complicated reality into functions with relatively simple mathematical properties. For example, the linear expenditure system[4] is a favourite choice for the demand, and the Cobb-Douglas or CES production function for the supply side.

Still another question is whether the end justifies the means. It should be borne in mind that the concept of effective protection was introduced to obtain a short-cut impression of the resource pulls and pushes among economic activities caused by the system of protection. Therefore effective-protection calculations should by nature be simple. Using a general-equilibrium model to solve secondary difficulties in effective protection calculations is like trying to hit a fly with a

1. See for example Evans (1972).
2. For a discussion of such models and their relation to other general-equilibrium models see Taylor and Lysy (1979).
3. See Dorfman et al. (1958), ch. 13.
4. A description of the main characteristics of the linear expenditure system can be found in Stone (1970). It was used for example in the income distribution model for South Korea by Adelman and Robinson (1977).

cricket bat and would render the effective-protection calculations themselves unnecessary.

6.1.4 Simplifying Assumptions

To avoid the complications implied by a general-equilibrium approach it is customary to make a simplifying assumption of the way the prices of the non-tradables respond to the elimination of the system of protection. Different possibilities are discussed in section 7.[5]

Throughout section 7 the calculations are assumed to be economy-wide and of the input-output type, along the lines set out in section 5.3. Moreover it is assumed that the distinction between tradable and non-tradable goods can be made to coincide with the sector classification of the table. In other words the sectors of the input-output table can be divided into a group of sectors exclusively producing tradables and another group exclusively producing non-tradables.

In practice there are always some sectors producing tradables and non-tradables at the same time. These sectors are usually classified according to their most important products and their nominal rates of protection are calculated on a sample in which the non-tradables are not represented. Such a procedure is not entirely justified but as long as the non-tradables do not have a great share in the production of these sectors, the errors are not expected to be significant. An example of how the production of non-tradables by sectors producing mainly tradables can be accounted for is given by Ten Kate.[6]

Finally it is assumed in the remainder of this chapter that there is no adjustment of the exchange rate to the free-trade situation. The implications of an exchange rate adjustment for the treatment of the non-tradables and the underlying assumptions are discussed in Chapter 7.

5. See also subsection 4.2.7.
6. Ten Kate et al. (1980), app. A, p. 278. Here the term 'global protection' is introduced to indicate protection given to a basket of both tradable and non-tradable goods.

6.2   Assumptions Regarding the Price Response of the Non-Tradables

6.2.1 The Original Balassa Method

In the original Balassa method[7] it is assumed that the prices of the non-tradables would not be affected by the elimination of the system of protection, that is, in the free-trade situation the non-tradables would assume prices equal to those holding in the protection situation. For the revaluation procedure of the input-output table described in subsection 5.3.3, this assumption implies that step 2 of the procedure can be omitted. This can be expressed by the following formula:

$$(6.1) \qquad W_N = 0 \quad \text{or} \quad V_N = \iota_N$$

where ι_N is again the row vector of units.

By substituting the deflators of the non-tradables according to (6.1) into the value-added at free-trade prices according to (5.15), the following expressions are obtained for the effective protection in absolute terms:

$$(6.2a) \qquad G_T^{OB} = Y_T - Y_T^{ft,OB} = (\iota_T - V_T)(\hat{X}_T - \hat{E}_T - A_{TT}) - (TI_T + TE_T)$$

$$(6.2b) \qquad G_N^{OB} = Y_N - Y_N^{ft,OB} = -(\iota_T - V_T) A_{TN} - (TI_N + TE_N)$$

and in relative terms:

$$(6.3a) \qquad Z_T^{OB} = G_T^{OB} (\hat{Y}_T^{ft,OB})^{-1}$$

$$(6.3b) \qquad Z_N^{OB} = G_N^{OB} (\hat{Y}_N^{ft,OB})^{-1}$$

where the superscript OB refers to the original Balassa method.

As long as positive nominal protection on the output for the

7. This revaluation device for the non-tradables(or rather non-revaluation device) was applied by Balassa (1965) in his study of protection for industrial countries. It is usually referred to as the Balassa method. To distinguish it from the Balassa method of later studies, it is called the original Balassa method.

domestic market $(\iota_T - V_T)$ $(\hat{X}_T - \hat{E}_T)$ outweighs the negative effects derived from input protection and foreign-trade taxation $(\iota_T - V_T)A_{TT} + (TI_T + TE_T)$, the effective protection of the tradables G_T^{OB} will result positive. The effective protection of the non-tradables will be negative, as a rule, owing to the normally positive protection of their tradable inputs.

This discrepancy between tradables and non-tradables represents at the same time the weakest point of the assumption adopted in this method. If, on the average, the sectors producing tradables benefit from the system of protection, why should the sectors producing non-tradables let themselves be discriminated against? The least they would do is to pass on the higher input costs to the price of their output. This latter behaviour is exactly the price response assumed in the modified Balassa method.

6.2.2 The Modified Balassa Method[8]

Here it is assumed that changes in input costs resulting from the elimination of the system of protection are passed on to the prices of the non-tradables. In other words it is no longer the prices of the non-tradables but the value-added generated with their production that is assumed to remain unaffected. Again it is recommended for reasons of uniformity to exclude exported output from such price adjustments, that is, the value of exported output of non-tradables does not change according to equation (5.12d).

Adopting the notation of Chapter 5, the assumption of the modified Balassa method can be written as follows:

$$(6.4) \qquad V_N \, (\hat{X}_N - \hat{E}_N) + E_N = V_T \, A_{TN} + V_N \, A_{NN} + M_N + TD_N + Y_N$$

The left-hand side of equation (6.4) stands for the value of the output at free-trade prices. The exported output (E_N) is not revalued while the output destined for the domestic market is revalued with the unknown deflators V_N. The right-hand side of the equation expresses the cost of production of the non-tradables as they would be in the free-trade

---

8. As in Balassa et al. (1971), app. A. In the literature it is also referred to as the Balassa method, but to avoid confusion it is here called the modified Balassa method.

situation. The fact that the value-added term Y_N is taken from the protection situation is characteristic of the modified Balassa method. It represents the assumption that the value-added is not affected by the elimination of the system of protection.

The system of equations (6.4) in the unknowns V_N can be solved by transferring the non-tradable input term $V_N A_{NN}$ to the left-hand side and inverting the Leontief-like flow matrix $(\hat{X}_N - \hat{E}_N - A_{NN})$:

$$(6.5) \qquad V_N = (V_T A_{TN} + M_N + TD_N + Y_N - E_N)(\hat{X}_N - \hat{E}_N - A_{NN})^{-1}$$

The row deflators V^N found in this way can now be applied in step 2 of the revaluation procedure of Chapter 5.

Substituting them in equations (5.15), the following expressions are obtained for the effective protection in absolute terms:

$$(6.6a) \qquad G_T^{MB} = (\iota_T - V_T)(\hat{X}_T - \hat{E}_T - A_{TT} - A_{TN} B_{NT}) - (TI_T + TE_T) - (TI_N + TE_N)B_{NT}$$

$$(6.6b) \qquad G_N^{MB} = 0$$

The matrix B_{NT} represents the backward linkages through intermediate demand of the sectors producing tradables with those producing non-tradables and are defined as:

$$(6.7) \qquad B_{NT} = (\hat{X}_N - \hat{E}_N - A_{NN})^{-1} A_{NT}$$

Not considering the special term for the export of non-tradables, expression (6.7) stands for the bunch concept in the semi-input-output sense[9]. The element of row k in column ℓ of the matrix B_{NT} expresses which part of the production of non-tradables k goes directly or indirectly into the production of tradeables ℓ.

Effective protection in relative terms is found by relating

9. The semi-input-output method was proposed by Tinbergen in the early sixties. See for example Tinbergen (1966). An extensive description is given by Kuyvenhoven (1978). The relation between the semi-input-output method and the assumptions regarding the price response of the non-tradables is spelt out by Ten Kate (1972).

absolute effective protection according to (6.6) to value added at free-
trade prices:

(6.8a) $Z_T^{MB} = G_T^{MB} \; (\hat{Y}_T^{ft,MB})^{-1}$

(6.8b) $Z_N^{MB} = 0$

Comparing the formulas for the effective protection obtained by the
two methods (6.2 and 6.6), it appears that the assumption of the
modified Balassa method moves a part of the negative effective
protection of the non-tradables (G_N^{OB}) to the tradables. As a result, the
average positive protection of the tradables decreases slightly, whereas
the negative protection of the non-tradables becomes zero. It should be
noted that only that part of the negative protection of the non-
tradables that corresponds to backward linkages with tradables is
shifted to the effective protection of the tradables. As explained below
(subsection 6.3.2), the remaining part is shifted to final demand.

Although the assumption of the modified Balassa method eliminates
the unrealistic negative effective protection of the non-tradables,
there still persists an important dissimilarity between sectors
producing tradables on the one hand and those producing non-tradables on
the other. While the former group receives positive protection on the
average, the effective protection of the latter, though not negative any
more, is zero.

In the two following methods this discrepancy between the two
groups of sectors is eliminated further. The assumptions regarding the
price response of the non-tradables bring the corresponding sectors on
to the same footing as the sectors producing tradables.

6.2.3 The Original Scott Method

In the original Scott method[10] it is assumed that nominal
protection to the non-tradables is uniform and equal to the average
nominal protection to the tradables, that is:

---

10. This method was suggested by Scott, in Little et al. (1970), ch.5.
    Here it is called the original Scott method to distinguish it from
    the modified method.

(6.9) $W_N = w^* \iota_N$ or $V_N = \dfrac{1}{1+w^*} \iota_N = v^* \iota_N$

where w^* is the average nominal protection given to the tradables.

It must be decided what sort of average should be taken. Several alternatives are at hand but the most reasonable option is to take a weighted average on domestic final demand for the tradables valued at free-trade prices, that is :

(6.10) $w^* = \dfrac{W_T DFD_T^{ft} + W_M M_F}{\iota_T DFD_T^{ft} + M_F}$

where W_M is defined as TI_F/M_F.

If the value of production is taken instead of domestic final demand, a well-known ambiguity is introduced in respect of the treatment of intra-sectoral deliveries, which can either be interpreted as a part of production, or not. Such ambiguities do not exist if domestic final demand is taken. Moreover the specific choice of the weights suggested above leads to some specific symmetry properties which are discussed in Chapter 8.

Substituting the deflators according to (6.9) in the definition of value-added at free-trade prices (5.15), the following expressions are obtained for the effective protection in absolute terms:

(6.11a) $G_T^{OS} = (\iota_T - V_T)(\hat{X}_T - \hat{E}_T - A_{TT}) - (1 - v^*) \iota_N A_{NT} - (TI_T + TE_T)$

(6.11b) $G_N^{OS} = (1 - v^*) \iota_N (\hat{X}_N - \hat{E}_N - A_{NN}) - (\iota_T - V_T) A_{TN} - (TI_N + TE_N)$

and in relative terms:

(6.12a) $Z_T^{OS} = G_T^{OS} (\hat{Y}_T^{ft,OS})^{-1}$

(6.12b) $Z_N^{OS} = G_N^{OS} (\hat{Y}_N^{ft,OS})^{-1}$

By raising nominal protection of the non-tradables to the average level of the tradables, effective protection of the sectors producing

non-tradables also increases considerably. For one sector it increases
more than for another, but on the average the effective protection of
the non-tradables is expected to come out at roughly the same level as
effective protection of the tradables. It should be noted that there is
a further decline of effective protection of the tradables because
nominal protection of their non-tradable inputs in the present method is
usually higher than in the modified Balassa method.

6.2.4 The Modified Scott Method

The Scott method can be modified in exactly the same way as the
Balassa method. Instead of nominal protection, now effective protection
of the non-tradables is assumed to be uniform and equal to the average
effective protection of the tradables. To the author's knowledge, such a
modification of the Scott method had never been mentioned explicitly in
the literature on protection until it was recently formulated by
Kuyvenhoven.[11]

The algebraic formulation of the modified Scott method is somewhat
more complicated than that of the modified Balassa method. As the
average effective protection of the tradables depends on the unknown
deflation indices for the non-tradables, the system of equations becomes
interdependent:

$$(6.13) \qquad V_N(\hat{X}_N - \hat{E}_N) + E_N = V_T A_{TN} + V_N A_{NN} + M_N + TD_N + Y_N(1 + z^*)^{-1}$$

$$(6.14) \qquad V_T(\hat{X}_T - \hat{E}_T) + E_T = V_T A_{TT} + V_N A_{NT} + M_T + TD_T + Y_T(I + Z_T)^{-1}$$

Equations (6.13 and 6.14) express the cost structure of the non-
tradables and the tradables respectively. The unknown average protection
z^* converts the value added of the non-tradables from protection to the
free-trade prices and should be equated to the average effective
protection of the tradables. The best way to do this is to take the
average on value-added at free-trade valuation:

$$(6.15) \qquad z^* = Y_T^{ft} Z_T / Y_T^{ft} \iota_T$$

11. See Kuyvenhoven (1978), p. 170.

From equation (6.15) it is easily verified that:

$$(6.16) \qquad (1 + z^*)^{-1} = Y_T \, (I + \hat{Z}_T)^{-1} \, \iota_T \, / \, Y_T \, \iota_T$$

Equations (6.13, 6.14 and 6.16) form a square system of linear equations in the unknowns V_N, $(I + \hat{Z}_T)^{-1} \, \iota_T$ and $(1 + z^*)^{-1}$. The special structure of the system permits the elimination of all unknowns except the deflators V_N's by summing up equation (6.14) over the sectors producing tradables and introducing the expression thus obtained for $Y_T \, (I + \hat{Z}_T)^{-1} \, \iota_T$ through (6.16) into equation (6.15). Solving the system is then a matter of matrix inversion.

Again the row deflators V_N obtained in this way can be introduced in the equation (5.15) and the expressions for effective protection according to the modified Scott method, G_T^{MS}, G_N^{MS}, Z_T^{MS} and Z_N^{MS}, can be derived. Although the derivation is straightforward, the rather long formulas are suppressed as they are not required for the understanding of the following.

The modification of the Scott method is not expected to change the spectrum of effective protection in a drastic way. Whereas in the original Scott method nominal protection of the non-tradables is uniform and effective protection is not, in the modified method the effective protection of the non-tradables is uniform and nominal protection is not, but the average levels of nominal and effective protection are hardly affected.

6.3   Incorporating Non-Tradable Inputs in the Value-Added

6.3.1 The Original Corden Method

It is also possible to give an entirely different treatment to the non-tradable inputs in the theory of effective protection. Instead of making specific assumptions about the price response of the non-tradables, Corden[12] has suggested incorporating the value of the non-tradable inputs into the value-added generated with the production of the tradables. The effective rate of protection is then obtained by applying definition (5.1) to this extended value-added concept.

---

12. This procedure was suggested by Corden (1966) and first applied
    empirically by Lewis and Guisinger (1968).

By doing so, the price response of the non-tradables is not relevant any more. Any price change of non-tradable inputs is compensated by an equivalent change of value added, the latter being obtained as a residue. Thus if non-tradable inputs and value-added are grouped together, the composite is obtained as a residue of output minus tradable inputs and the price response of the non-tradables no longer plays a role.

Using the notation introduced in Chapter 5, the composite value added CY can be written as:

(6.17a) $CY_T^{OC} = Y_T + \iota_N A_{NT} = X_T - \iota_T A_{TT} - M_T - IT_T$

(6.17b) $CY_T^{ft,OC} = Y_T^{ft} + \iota_N A_{NT}^{ft} = V_T (\hat{X}_T - \hat{E}_T - A_{TT}) + E_T - M_T - TD_T$

where equations (6.17a and b) express the composite value-added at protection and free-trade prices respectively. The effective protection according to the original Corden method can now be written as:

(6.18) $G_T^{OC} = CY_T^{OC} - CY_T^{ft,OC} = (\iota_T - V_T)(\hat{X}_T - \hat{E}_T - A_{TT}) - (TI_T + TE_T)$

and in relative terms:

(6.19) $Z_T^{OC} = G_T^{OC} (\hat{CY}_T^{ft,OC})^{-1}$

It is interesting to see that the effective protection in absolute terms according to this method is exactly equal to that of the original Balassa method. The effective rates of protection differ between the two methods only because the denominator now includes the value of non-tradable inputs.

It should be noted that in the Corden method there is no effective rate of protection for the non-tradables. In the other methods it is not an important issue either. It rather appears as a byproduct of the assumptions regarding the price response of the non-tradables. Therefore the resulting effective rates are very sensitive to the assumption made and no firm conclusions can be based upon them. In the Corden method however the effective protection given to the non-tradables is channelled through the sectors producing tradables. More precisely,

effective protection of tradables does not apply exclusively to the
sectors themselves but incorporates an element of protection to their
backward linkages with sectors producing non-tradables.

6.3.2 The Modified Corden Method

The modified Corden method[13] attempts to make this interpretation
more explicit. This method assumes that the complete value of the non-
tradable inputs is not incorporated in the value-added of the tradables,
but only their direct and indirect value-added content. More precisely:
every non-tradable input is decomposed following its cost composition
into a value-added part and its different tradable-input parts. This
decomposition is performed in a cumulative manner. That is, any non-
tradable input part appearing in the decomposition is decomposed again
so that at last there is a decomposition into value-added and tradable
inputs only.

This procedure can be illustrated by a contraction of the input-
output table to a new table of smaller size. In the reduced table, all
sectors producing non-tradables are eliminated and their deliveries to
the other sectors and to final demand are decomposed and reallocated to
the corresponding rows of value added and tradable inputs according to
the lines set out above.

Taking the input-output table at protection prices (Table 5.1) as a
starting point, this reallocation of non-tradable inputs and final
deliveries leads to the following contracted table:

13. The modified Corden method was suggested in the same article as the
    original Corden method, albeit in a footnote. See Corden (1966).
    Corden (1971) worked it out in more detail. An algebraic statement
    of the method is given by Balassa et al. (1971).

Table 6.1   Contracted Input-Output Table: at real prices

Sectors	Tradables	Exports	Domestic Fin.Dem.	Total
Tradables	$A_{TT} + A_{TN}B_{NT}$	E_T	$DFD_T + A_{TN}B_{NF}$	X_T
Imports	$M_T + (M_N-E_N)B_{NT}$	$E_N{}^1{}_N$	$M_F + (M_N-E_N)B_{NF}$	M_{TOT}
Ind.Taxes	$IT_T + IT_N B_{NT}$	IT_E	$IT_F + IT_N B_{NF}$	IT_{TOT}
Value-Added	$Y_T + Y_N B_{NT}$	–	$Y_G + Y_N B_{NF}$	Y_{TOT}
Total	X_T	E_{TOT}	DFD_{TOT}	

In this table the bunches B_{NF} are defined in a similar way as the bunches B_{NT} of formula (6.7):

$$(6.20) \qquad B_{NF} = (\hat{X}_N - \hat{E}_N - A_{NN})^{-1} DFD_N$$

That is, the bunches indicate which part of the total production of the non-tradables for the domestic market $(X_N - E_N)$ goes directly or indirectly to each of the categories of the domestic final demand.

In the contracted table the rows and columns corresponding to the non-tradables have disappeared. The non-tradable inputs in the tradables A_{NT} have been decomposed into indirect tradable inputs $A_{TN}B_{NT}$, indirect net imports $(M_N - E_N)B_{NT}$, indirect net-indirect taxes $IT_N B_{NT}$ and indirect value added $Y_N B_{NT}$. It is easily verified in this way that the non-tradable inputs A_{NT} are exactly accounted for in each column. In other words the column sums X_T remain the same.

In a similar way the non-tradable deliveries to domestic final demand DFD_D are decomposed into tradable inputs $A_{TN}B_{NF}$, net imports $(M_N - E_N)B_F$, indirect taxes $IT_N B_{NF}$ and value added $Y_N B_{NF}$. Again it can easily be proven that the column sums DFD_{TOT} remain intact.

It is interesting that this special way of contracting the input-output table not only leads to unchanged column totals, but the row totals do not change either.

To that end we only had to shift the exports of non-tradables to the
import row in order not to lose them from the export column and to
compensate for them as negative costs.[14]

Effective protection according to the modified Corden method can
now be calculated by applying the consecutive steps of revaluation in
Chapter 5 to the contracted table. As the non-tradables have been
eliminated their revaluation is no longer a problem. The composite value
added has been reduced so as to include only the value-added part of the
non-tradable inputs:

$$(6.21) \qquad CY_T^{MC} = Y_T + Y_N B_{NT}$$

The revaluation procedure with row deflators V_T and indirect-tax
prescriptions TD_T and TD_N for the free-trade situation leads to the
following expression for effective protection:

$$(6.22) \qquad G_T^{MC} = CY_T^{MC} - CY_T^{ft,MC} = (\iota_T - V_T)(\hat{X}_T - \hat{E}_T - A_{TT} - A_{TN} B_{NT}) +$$

$$- (TI_T + TE_T) - (TI_N + TE_N) B_{NT}$$

and in relative terms:

$$(6.23) \qquad Z_T^{MC} = G_T^{MC} (\hat{CY}_T^{ft,MC})^{-1}$$

Again it is interesting to note that effective protection in absolute
terms according to the modified Corden method is exactly equal to that
according to the modified Balassa-method (6.6a). Thus if the
corresponding effective rates are different, this is brought about by
the difference in the denominator. As the composite value-added is
always larger than the direct value-added the effective rate according
to the modified Corden method is always smaller in absolute value than
the modified Balassa rate, at least if the value-added is not negative

14. To keep overall consistency, it is necessary to treat the
contradictory exports of non-tradables as negative costs. This is
because these exports are not revalued. If they are revalued in
the same way as domestic sales, it is not necessary to treat them
as negative costs and the contraction of the input-output table
can be adjusted accordingly.

under free trade.

6.4   Contribution of Non-Tradable Inputs to Effective Protection

6.4.1 Introductory Remarks

The starting point of the discussion is Table 5.3 where effective
protection is decomposed into protection of output on the one hand, and
protection on different kinds of inputs on the other. It should be noted
that a number of the entries of the decomposition table do not depend on
the sort of treatment that is given to the non-tradables. Only the
entries for non-tradables themselves change from one method to another.

This section focuses on the contribution of non-tradable-input
protection to the effective protection of the tradables. In the
decomposition table this contribution is represented by the block of
entries in the intersection of the non-tradable input rows with the
columns for the sectors producing tradables: $(I-\hat{V}_N) A_{NT}$. Its values can
be calculated according to any of the above methods by substituting the
corresponding characteristic expression for the non-tradable deflators
V_N. In the original Balassa method, for example, all entries will be
zero as there is no deflation of non-tradable flows. In all other
methods, there is a non-zero contribution.

The elaboration of the formulas for the alternative methods is
straight-forward and is not given here. The following subsections pay
some attention to the interpretation of the methods. Two cases in
particular are considered: the modified Balassa method and the modified
Corden method. It is shown that the modified Balassa method classifies
the protection derived from the non-tradables according to the kind of
non-tradable inputs, whereas in the modified Corden method this
protection is classified according to the kind of tradable inputs
indirectly linked with the non-tradables.

6.4.2 Decomposition according to Non-Tradable Inputs

In the modified Balassa method the non-tradables are revalued with
the row deflators from formula (6.5) and the contribution of the non-
tradables to the effective protection of the tradables $(I - \hat{V}_N) A_{NT}$
appears in the corresponding column of the decomposition table. Now the
question is, what do the individual entries of this column stand for?

Let us consider electricity as a non-tradable input[15] and focus on the entries in the corresponding row of the decomposition table. It is assumed that fuel oils which represent the main tradable inputs of the electricity sector are negatively protected, that is they are cheaper in the domestic market than in the international market. In this way the electricity sector receives effective protection on cheap fuel inputs. But the modified Balassa method assumes that this protection is passed on to the price of the final product, electricity in this case. Thus electricity is also cheaper than it would have been under free-trade conditions. That means that all sectors using electricity as an intermediate input receive protection brought about by the cheaper fuel oils indirectly through their electricity inputs. That sort of protection is contained in the electricity row of the decomposition table.

Not only fuel oils, but also other tradable inputs may generate effective protection for the electricity sector, either directly or indirectly through the other non-tradables. In the modified Balassa method this protection is also passed on to the electricity users. Thus it is also contained in the flows of the electricity row.

In other words, under the modified Balassa method all protection (positive or negative) entering through electricity as an input is channelled through the electricity row of the decomposition table irrespective of the sort of tradable inputs by which it is caused. But as subsection 6.4.3. explains, in the modified Corden method it is the sort of indirect tradable input that determines the classification.

6.4.3 Decomposition according to Indirect Tradable Inputs

It should be remembered that effective protection in absolute terms according to the modified Corden method is equal to that under the assumptions of the modified Balassa method.[16] As a consequence the protection derived from the non-tradable inputs, considered in subsection 6.4.2, must still be present somewhere in the decomposition table of the modified Corden method.

---

15. Up to a certain extent electricity is tradable, but so much power is lost transporting it over long distances that it is commonly treated as a non-tradable.
16. See section 6.3.2.

However this method works with the contracted table, from which the rows and columns corresponding with the non-tradables have been removed. In the contracted decomposition table negative effective protection derived from tradable inputs can be written as:

$$(6.24) \quad - G_{TT} = (I - \hat{V}_T) A_{TT} + (I - \hat{V}_T) A_{TN} B_{NT}$$

The first term on the right-hand side corresponds with effective protectiondirectly derived from the tradable inputs. It does not depend on the specific treatment given to the non-tradables and forms part of the decomposition table of any of the methods here discussed.

The second term is characteristic of the modified Corden method. It represents effective protection of the tradables slipping in indirectly through the non-tradables and corresponds to the column of entries in the non-tradable rows of the decomposition table discussed in section 6.3 . It is easily verified that, together with a similar second term in the indirect-tax row of the contracted table, their total contribution is equal to the sum of the entries in the non-tradable block of the uncontracted table. The difference is in the arrangement.

To give an example, let us return to the comparatively cheap fuel oils. In the modified Balassa method the resulting protection for the electricity sector is passed on to the electricity consumers and put in the electricity row. In the present method, irrespective of whether or not it is passed on, this protection remains in the tradable row of fuel oils and is grouped together with the direct-input protection of the first term of (6.24). Moreover not only the protection given to the electricity inputs but also that given to all other non-tradable inputs (transport margins, for instance) are put in the same entry. Thus in general terms the contribution of the non-tradables inputs to the effective protection of the tradables is traced back to its tradable prime cause and is classified accordingly.

6.5   Concluding Remarks

6.5.1 The Exports of Non-Tradables: a nuisance

It must be said that the presentation of the methods given here is slightly different from the usual forms: and the difference is precisely in the treatment of the contradictory exports of non-tradables.

In this chapter the exports of non-tradables are treated essentially as negative costs to the corresponding sectors.The negative entry E_N is introduced into a number of formulas where it would be absent in the customary formulation. By so doing it keeps the revaluation of the export column uniform and therefore the national accounting identities and the rules governing average nominal and effective protection can retain the simple form obtained in section 5.4.

It is equally possible however to revaluate the exports of the non-tradables with the nominal rate of protection V_N applicable to domestic sales. The methods would then coincide exactly with the conventions in the literature. It is easily verified that the implied changes consist of the suppression of all terms E_N in equations (6.4, 5, 7, 13 and 20). Also the contraction of the input-output table as proposed in subsection 6.3.2 can be maintained, if the exports of non-tradables E_N are no longer moved to the import row and compensated for as negative costs, but directly distributed over the export column as done with the non-tradable deliveries to the tradables and to final demand. The disadvantage would be that the averaging rules would have to include the somewhat arbitrary term $(I - \hat{V}_N) E_N$. As the exports of non-tradables are usually small, there is hardly any difference in quantitative outcomes between one formulation and the other.

6.5.2 Theoretical Comparison of the Methods

Comparing the alternative treatments of the non-tradables from a theoretical point of view, it may be concluded that the assumptions of the price response of the non-tradables to the elimination of the foreign-trade regime are most realistic in the original and modified Balassa and the Scott methods.

The Corden methods add nothing new to the Balassa methods where effective protection in absolute terms is concerned. The only difference is that in the Corden methods effective protection to the sectors producing tradables is extended to their backward linkages with the sectors producing non-tradables, whereas in the Balassa methods effective protection applies only to the sectors producing tradeables.

Thus the effective rates according to the Corden methods take account of the inertia caused by heavy backward linkages with the non-tradables. More precisely, sectors that are heavily dependent on non-tradable inputs need more effective protection relative to their own value-added in order to receive the same incentives as sectors less dependent on non-tradable inputs. So it is not surprising that in general-equilibrium models the Corden effective rates do better in predicting movements in resource reallocation among sectors producing tradables than the Balassa or the Scott effective rates.[17]

On the other hand the Corden effective rates have the disadvantage that they do not apply to individual sectors but to a complicated mixture of interdependent productive activities which cannot be identified so easily. In the other methods the effective rate of protection refers to one single sector while the protection given to the bunch of backward linkages with the non-tradables is taken care of by the specific price response assumed for the non-tradables.

Moreover the price behaviour of the non-tradables assumed in the modified Balassa method is interesting in itself, apart from calculations of effective protection. It is similar to that proposed by Little and Mirrlees[18] for purposes of project evaluation and permits the identification of the sources of effective protection as described in section 6.4.

6.5.3 Empirical Comparison of the Methods

In spite of the differences in mathematical complexity, generally the alternative methods do not lead to substantially different quantitative results. Evidently as a result of the different assumptions of the price response of the non-tradables, the effective rates of protection for these goods vary considerably from one method to another. It should be realised however that the effective protection of the non-tradables is of a hypothetical nature and should rather be considered as a byproduct of the effective protection of the tradables.

The effective protection of the tradables is not very sensitive to changes in the treatment of the non-tradables. There is particularly

17. Results of this nature were reported by Ray (1973) and Suzuki (1979).
18. See Little and Mirrlees (1974), ch.12; and Squire and Van der Tak (1975), ch.9 and 12.

little difference between the results of the original methods and those
of the corresponding modified methods. This is clearly demonstrated by
the results brought together in Table 6.14, where the protective rates
found in the numerical example are compared. The difference between the
Balassa and the Scott methods is somewhat more pronounced but still not
very important in the light of the uncertainties of the measurement of
the nominal rates of protection. Only the Corden methods lead to substantially different effective rates, but that is due to the reasons
explained in the subsection 6.5.2.

     With these observations in mind, it is questionable whether the
presumed improvement resulting from the modification of any of the
original methods justifies the implied mathematical complications.
Generally, for those only interested in the intersector structure of
effective protection, the treatment given to the non-tradables is not of
great importance. However for those more specifically interested in
distortions in the valuation of the non-tradables brought about by the
system of protection or in the way in which input protection may be
passed on by the sectors producing non-tradables, the modified Balassa,
Scott and Corden methods are useful analytical tools.

6.6   Numerical Example

6.6.1 The Modified Balassa Method

     In the numerical example of Chapter 5, the assumption of the
original Balassa method was adopted. Here effective protection is
calculated under the other assumptions discussed above. First the
modified Balassa method is applied.

     In calculating the price deflators for the non-tradables V_N with
equation (6.5), the third and the fourth rows must be multiplied by deflators 0.9718 and 0.9734 respectively. Applying the revaluation steps
to the input-output table at basic prices (Table 5.6) but including the
revaluation of the non-tradables, the following table at free-trade
prices is obtained:

Table 6.2   Input-Output Table: values at free-trade prices
            (according to the modified Balassa method)

Sectors	1	2	3	4	Sub-total	Ex-ports	Domestic Fin.Dem	Total
1. Primary	285	661	-	93	1039	413	1284	2736
2. Industry	193	407	80	221	901	333	786	2020
3. Trade	114	143	127	135	519	108	659	1286
4. Others	112	124	236	310	782	-	1973	2755
Subtotal	704	1335	443	759	3241	854	4702	8797
5. Imports	133	212	54	61	460	-	751	1211
6. Ind.Taxes	41	58	22	30	151	-	161	312
7.Value Added	1858	415	767	1905	4945	-	-	4945
Total	2736	2020	1286	2755	8797	854	5614	

A good deal of this table coincides with the corresponding table of the
original Balassa method. The first two rows, for example, have been
deflated with the same nominal protection and thus coincide exactly with
those of table 5.7. This also applies to the import row and the row of
indirect taxes. But contrary to the original Balassa method, rows 3 and
4 have been deflated and thus also the totals of columns 3 and
4.Consequently the value-added at free-trade prices of sectors 1 and 2
has become somewhat higher while that of sectors 3 and 4 has been
brought back to the levels they had in the protection situation.
Comparison with the table at protection prices leads to the following
results in terms of effective protection.

Table 6.3   Effective Protection by Sector
            (according to the modified Balassa method)

Sectors	Value-Added at with protection	Factor Costs under free trade	Effective Protection: Difference	Effective rate of protection %
1. Primary	1731	1858	- 127	- 6.8
2. Industry	727	415	312	75.2
3. Trade	767	767	0	0.0
4. Other	1905	1905	0	0.0
Total	5130	4945	185	3.7

The assumption of the modified Balassa method is recognised in the zero
effective protection for the non-tradables. The effective rates for the
tradables are slightly lower than in the original method.

In the same way as before, effective protection can be decomposed
into output and input protection.

Table 6.4   Decomposition of Effective Protection
            (according to the modified Balassa method)

Sources	1	2	3	4	Sub-total	Ex-ports	Domestic Fin.Dem.	Total
a. Output	-47	421	34	76	484	-	349	833
b. Inputs	80	109	34	76	299	-	349	648
1. Primary	(-6)	(-13)	(-)	(-2)	(-21)	-	(-26)	(-47)
2. Industry	(48)	(102)	(20)	(55)	(225)	-	(196)	(421)
3. Trade	(3)	(4)	(4)	(4)	(15)	-	(19)	(34)
4. Others	(3)	(3)	(6)	(9)	(21)	-	(55)	(76)
5. Imports	(-)	(-)	(-)	(-)	(-)	-	(-)	(-)
6. Ind.Taxes	(32)	(13)	(4)	(10)	(59)	-	(105)	(164)
c.Effective Protection	-127	312	-	-	185	-	-	185

The flow of 4 million in column 2 under the inputs from the trade sector
has the following meaning. As a result of input protection and indirect
taxation, the services of the trade sector are more expensive in reality

than they would have been under free trade. The 4 million entry
expresses what the industrial sector is additionally spending on those
services.

As far as the national accounting identities are concerned, nominal
protection on domestic final demand amounts to 349 million which is
counter-balanced by 185 million of effective protection to the
productive sectors and another 164 million of indirect taxation to the
tax collector.

6.6.2 The Original Scott Method

In this method price deflation of the non-tradables is uniform and
is calculated with formula (6.10). This leads to a deflation factor of
0.9025 and the following input-output table at free-trade prices is
found:

Table 6.5   Input-Output Table: values at free-trade prices
            (according to the original Scott method)

Sectors	1	2	3	4	Sub-total	Ex-ports	Domestic Fin.Dem.	Total
1. Primary	285	661	-	93	1039	413	1284	2736
2. Industry	193	407	80	221	901	333	786	2020
3. Trade	106	133	118	125	482	108	612	1202
4. Others	104	115	218	288	725	-	1830	2555
Subtotal	688	1 316	416	727	3147	854	4512	8513
5. Imports	133	212	54	61	460	-	751	1211
6. Ind.Taxes	41	58	22	30	151	-	161	312
7.Value Added	1874	434	710	1737	4755	-	-	4755
Total	2736	2 020	1202	2 555	8513	854	5424	-

The deflation of the non-tradables is stronger than the assumption of
the modified Balassa method. As a consequence the effective protection
to the tradables declines further, while that to the non-tradables
becomes positive. The results are presented in the following table:

Table 6.6   Effective Protection by Sector
            (according to the original Scott method)

Sectors	Value-Added at Factor Costs with protection	under free-trade	Effective Protection: Difference	Effective rate of protection %
1. Primary	1731	1874	- 143	- 7.6
2. Industry	727	434	293	67.5
3. Trade	767	710	57	8.0
4. Other	1905	1737	168	9.7
Total	5130	4755	375	7.9 %

The uniform revaluation of the non-tradables has led to an effective
rate of protection for sector 4 somewhat higher than that of sector 3.
In the modified Scott method which is calculated in the next subsection,
it is the effective protection that becomes uniform. This is achieved by
slightly different deflators for rows 3 and 4.

6.6.3 The Modified Scott Method

Solving the system of equations (6.13, 6.14 and 6.16) leads to
the following solution for the non-tradable-row deflators V_N and for the
average effective protection z^*:

$$z^* = 0.0684$$
$$v_3 = 0.9148$$
$$v_4 = 0.9216$$

With the uniform revaluation of the original Scott method, the effective
rate of sector 4 results somewhat higher than that of sector 3.
Therefore it is not surprising that in order to arrive at a uniform
effective protection for the non-tradables the deflation of row 4 must
be somewhat weaker than that of row 3.

Introducing these values for v_3 and v_4 into the revaluation
procedure obtains the following table at free-trade prices:

Table 6.7   Input-Output Table: values at free-trade prices
            (according to the modified Scott method)

Sectors	1	2	3	4	Sub-total	Ex-ports	Domestic Fin.Dem.	Total
1. Primary	285	661	-	93	1039	413	1284	2736
2. Industry	193	407	80	221	901	333	786	2020
3. Trade	107	134	120	127	488	108	621	1217
4. Others	106	117	223	294	740	-	1869	2609
Subtotal	691	1319	423	735	3168	854	4560	8582
5. Imports	133	212	54	61	460	-	751	1211
6. Ind.Taxes	41	58	22	30	151	-	161	312
7.Value-Added	1871	431	718	1783	4803	-	-	4803
Total	2736	2020	1217	2609	8582	854	5472	-

As a result of the weaker row deflation in comparison with the original
method, particularly for sector 4, effective protection declines to 6.8
per cent for both sectors producing non-tradables. The results are
brought together in Table 6.8.

Table 6.8   Effective Protection by Sector
            (according to the modified Scott method)

Sectors	Value-Added at Factor Costs with protection	under free-trade	Effective Protection: Difference	Effective rate of protection %
1. Primary	1731	1871	- 140	- 7.5
2. Industry	727	431	296	68.7
3. Trade	767	718	49	6.8
4. Other	1905	1783	122	6.8
Total	5130	4803	327	6.8

As the uniform effective protection of the non-tradables is put equal to
the average effective protection of the tradables, average effective
protection of all productive sectors also results at the same level of
6.8 per cent.

In both the original and modified Scott methods effective
protection can be decomposed in exactly the same way as in the Balassa
methods and it is easily verified that the overall balancing indentities
are again fulfilled . To avoid an unnecessary multitude of numerical
material, the corresponding tables are suppressed.

6.6.4 The Original Corden Method

The Corden methods are not characterised by any specific deflation
device for the non-tradables but by the composite-value-added concepts
of formulas (6.17) and (6.21). In the original Corden method the full
value of non-tradable inputs is incorporated in the value-added. The
results in terms of effective protection are summarised in Table 6.9:

Table 6.9   Effective Protection by Sector
            (according to the original Corden method)

Sectors	Value-Added* at with protection	Factor Costs under free-trade	Effective Protection: Difference	Effective rate of protection %
1. Primary	1963	2084	- 121	- 5.8
2. Industry	1001	682	319	46.8
Total	2964	2766	198	7.2

* Composite value-added according to formula (6.17)

The composite value-added of the protection situation is calculated from
Table 5.6. The composite value-added at free-trade prices is obtained
from Table 5.7, which corresponds to the original Balassa method.Exactly
the same figures are obtained if they are calculated from any of the
other tables at free-trade prices (Tables 6.2, 6.5 or 6.7).

6.6.5 The Modified Corden Method

First the input-output table at protection prices (Table 5.6) is
contracted according to the methodology set out in subsection 6.3.2.
This leads to the following contracted input-output table in which the
flows are decomposed into their direct and indirect components:

Table 6.10   Contracted Input-Output Table: at protection prices
             (according to the modified Corden method)

Sectors		1	2	Ex-ports	Domestic Fin.Dem.	Total
1. Primary :	direct	279	648	413	1258	2598
	indirect	5	6	-	80	91
	total	284	654	413	1338	2689
2. Industry:	direct	241	509	333	982	2065
	indirect	28	32	-	316	376
	total	269	541	333	1 298	2441
3. Imports :	direct	133	212	-	751	1096
	indirect	-3	-4	108	14	115
	total	130	208	108	765	1211
4. Indirect	direct	73	71	-	266	410
Taxes:	indirect	5	6	-	55	66
	total	78	77	-	321	476
5. Value	direct	1731	727	-	-	2458
Added	indirect	197	234	-	2241	2672
	total	1928	961	-	2241	5130
Total		2689	2441	854	5963	-

It is interesting that the rows and columns of the non-tradables have
been internalised in such a way that all remaining rows and columns keep
their original totals. The negative entries in the indirect part of the
import row are due to the fact that exports of sector 3 are accounted
for as negative costs.

As the non-tradables have disappeared from the contracted Table,
Table 6.10 can be converted to free-trade valuation without any specific
revaluation device for the non-tradables. By so doing the following
contracted table at free-trade prices is obtained:

Table 6.11   Contracted Input-Output Table: at free trade prices
             (according to the modified Corden method)

Sectors		1	2	Ex-ports	Domestic Fin.Dem.	Total
1. Primary :	direct	285	661	41	1284	2643
	indirect	5	6	-	82	93
	total	290	667	413	1366	2736
2. Industry:	direct	193	407	333	786	1719
	indirect	22	26	-	253	301
	total	215	433	333	1039	2020
3. Imports :	direct	133	212	-	751	1096
	indirect	-3	-4	108	14	115
	total	130	208	108	765	1211
4. Indirect	direct	41	58	-	161	260
Taxes:	indirect	4	5	-	43	52
	total	45	63	-	204	312
5. Value Added		2056	649	-	-	-
Total		2736	2020	854	-	-

Table 6.11 is obtained by revaluation of Table 6.10 at free-trade
prices. It can also be obtained by contracting one of the tables at
free-trade prices (Tables 6.2, 6.5 or 6.7) according to the rules set
out in subsection 6.3.2. It is notable that any of these free-trade
tables, irrespective of the sort of price response assumed for the non-
tradables, leads to the same contracted table. The only difference
between one contracted table and another would be in the way the
composite value-added is split up in its direct and indirect parts. As
the composite value-added of Table 6.11 is obtained as a residue it is
not divided into direct and indirect components. The value-added part of
domestic final demand is not been supplied because it is the only flow
of the contracted table that would depend upon the specific price
response assumed for the non-tradables.

Table 6.12   Effective Protection by Sector
             (according to the modified Corden method)

Sectors	Value-Added* at with protection	Factor Costs under free trade	Effective Protection: Difference	Effective rate of protection
1. Primary	1928	056	-128	- 6.2 %
2. Industry	961	649	312	48.1 %
Total	2889	2705	184	6.8 %

* Composite value-added according to formula (6.21)

The effective protection found by comparing Tables 6.10 and 6.11 is given in Table 6.12. As in this method only the value-added part of the non-tradable inputs is incorporated, the composite value-added results somewhat lower than that of Table 6.9 where the full value of non-tradable inputs is included. In absolute terms effective protection coincides with that of the modified Balassa method (Table 6.3),[19] as it should be according to formulas (6.6a) and (6.22).

A final point to note is that the average effective protection in relative terms of 6.8 per cent coincides with that of the modified Scott method. It can be demonstrated that this is not a mere coincidence but follows the fact that the composite value-added at free-trade prices does not depend upon the treatment given to the non-tradables. Therefore, contracting the free-trade table of the modified Scott method where average effective protection of the tradables combined with whatever part of the non-tradables is equal to z^*, must necessarily lead to an average effective protection to the composite value-added of the same magnitude. Changing the assumption of the price response of the non-tradables shifts effective protection between the direct and indirect components but cannot affect average effective protection to composite value-added.

As effective protection in absolute terms is the same in the modified Balassa and Corden methods, it is of interest to compare their

19. The difference of one unit in the primary sector is due to rounding.

decomposition tables.Table 6.13 according to the modified Corden method
is set against Table 6.4 (modified Balassa). In the latter the effective
protection of industry due to non-tradable inputs is minus 7 million,of
which 4 million is derived from the trade sector, the remaining 3
million from sector 4. In Table 6.13 the same 7 million appear as
indirect-input protection in the second column, but this protection is
now allocated to the corresponding tradable-input rows: 6 million stem
from indirect industrial inputs and the remaining 1 million from
indirect taxation of imported inputs in the non-tradables. Similar
observations can be made in respect of the first column and of domestic
final demand, where the difference of 1 million is due to rounding.

Table 6.13   Decomposition of Effective Protection
             (according to the modified Corden method)

	1	2	Ex-ports	Domestic Fin.Dem.	Total
a. Output	-47	421	-	348	722
b. Inputs*	81 (7)	109 (7)	-	348 (73)	538 (87)
1. Primary	-6 (-)	-13 (-)	-	-28 (-2)	-47 (-2)
2. Industry	54 (6)	108 (6)	-	259 (63)	421 (75)
5. Imports	-	-	-	-	-
6. Ind.Taxes	33 (1)	14 (1)	-	117 (12)	164 (14)
c. Effective Protection	-128	312	-	-	184

* The figures within parentheses indicate the indirect part.

6.6.6 Comparison of the Methods[20]
     In Table 6.14 nominal and effective protection according to the
alternative treatments of the non-tradables are brought together.
Nominal protection of the tradables is the same in all methods. The
nominal protection of the non-tradables reflects the assumption that
their prices respond to the elimination of the foreign-trade regime.

20. See also subsection 6.5.2.

Table 6.14 Nominal and Effective Protection: comparative results

Protection	Balassa Method		Scott Method		Corden Method	
	Original	Modified	Original	Modified	Original	Modified
Nominal Protective Rates						
1. Primary	-2.0	-2.0	-2.0	-2.0	-2.0	-2.0
2. Industry	25.0	25.0	25.0	25.0	25.0	25.0
3. Trade	0.0	2.8	9.7	9.3	-	-
4. Others	0.0	2.7	9.7	8.5	-	-
Effective Protection (Absolute)						
1. Primary	-121	-127	-143	-140	-121	-128
2. Industry	319	312	293	296	319	312
3. Trade	-24	0	57	49	-	-
4. Others	-63	0	168	122	-	-
Effective Protective Rates (%)						
1. Primary	-6.5	-6.8	-7.6	-7.5	-5.8	-6.2
2. Industry	78.2	75.2	67.5	68.7	46.8	48.1
3. Trade	-3.0	0.0	8.0	6.8	-	-
4. Others	-3.2	0.0	9.7	6.8	-	-

Both Corden methods lead to effective rates of protection substantially lower (in absolute value) than the other methods. It is again stressed however that effective protection in absolute terms is exactly equal in the Corden and the Balassa methods: the difference is only that in the Corden methods the same protection is no longer related to the value-added of the tradables but to the extended concept which incorporates the backward linkages with the non-tradables.

7 Exchange rate adjustment

7.1 The Free-Trade Exchange Rate

7.1.1 Introductory Remarks

Throughout the input-output calculations of effective protection presented in the previous chapters, the exchange rate of the protection situation was assumed to persist under free-trade conditions. This assumption was to avoid unnecessarily complicating the exposition: but there are hardly any arguments in its support. On the contrary, it is unlikely that with the elimination of the system of protection the existing exchange rate could be maintained. As most foreign-trade regimes are more restrictive on the import than the export side - if they are at all restrictive on the export side - the increase in imports following the elimination of import tariffs and licences would not be offset by an equivalent increase in export earnings. Consequently the commodity balance of the country would deteriorate, which under ceteris-paribus conditions could only be remedied by an adjustment of the exchange rate. In this present section therefore attention is focused on the free-trade exchange rate, that is, the rate of exchange that would bring back the balance of payments to its original equilibrium.

A few words about what is meant by 'equilibrium of the balance of payments' seem to be in order. As a balance of payments is nothing more than a double entry account of a country's transactions abroad, the overall balance of payments is in equilibrium by definition. The expression 'disequilibrium of the balance of payments' is then supposed to mean that transactions in the real sphere do not balance and corrective measures in the monetary sphere are required to close the account. It is not intended to join the debate on what exactly should be considered 'above the line' or 'below': here the balance of payments is said to be in equilibrium if there are neither sudden and unplanned changes in the reserves nor short-term capital movements. That is, the balance on the current account is allowed to be in deficit (or surplus) as long as it is compensated by long-term capital movements.

All the same, with these global specifications there is room for disagreement. It is often difficult to decide whether a balance of payments is in equilibrium or, if it is not, to define the extent of disequilibrium.

Apart from these ambiguities there are other factors preventing a precise estimation of the free-trade exchange rate. Even though this subject has been a focus of interest to economists and financiers ever since balances of payments have been in disequilibrium, it has not been possible to develop satisfactory models of exchange rate determination with a broad application range. With that in mind it would be unrealistic to expect a precise estimation of what the exchange rate would be under conditions of free trade. Error margins of a few per cent seem to be unavoidable and any estimate claiming a higher precision would at least be suspicious.

In the remainder of this section, the definition of the free-trade exchange rate is refined further. Attention is paid to the possibility that the balance of payments is in disequilibrium in the protection situation and the relation between an actual devaluation to remedy such a disequilibrium and the exchange rate adjustment in the protection context is discussed.In section 7.2 two alternative methods to estimate the free-trade exchange rate are set out.

7.1.2 The Free-Trade Exchange Rate

The free-trade exchange rate is the rate of exchange at which the balance of payments would be in equilibrium in the free-trade situation. It must be pointed out that the exchange rate that brings about a special type of equilibrium on the balance of payments does not only depend on the particular foreign-trade regime in force but also on other components of economic policy, particularly monetary and fiscal policies. Balassa and Schydlowsky[1] observe rightly that 'there are an infinite number of "equilibrium" exchange rates, each corresponding to a different configuration of trade, monetary, and fiscal policies'. Following their argument, the free-trade exchange rate must be defined as the one obtained under ceteris-paribus conditions, that is, without altering other elements of economic policy.

Unfortunately it is not possible to suppress the system of

1. See Balassa and Schydlowsky (1968), p. 357.

protection without affecting fiscal policies because part of the system
is fiscal by nature. The tariff revenues forgone by the government in
the free-trade situation will affect the internal balance of the
country, which may call for counteractive measures in the fiscal and/or
monetary sphere. But still, as only on rare occasions tariff revenues
form a substantial part of total tax revenues, ignoring these side
effects does not seem unreasonable. If on the other hand, together with
the system of protection, the entire indirect-tax system is also
eliminated,[2] this problem would deserve somewhat more attention than it
usually receives.

The impact of the system of protection on the balance of payments
mainly operates through the commodity balance. Thus if the system of
protection is eliminated while other elements of economic policy remain
unchanged it is in the first place the commodity balance which is
affected. This does not imply that other entries may not be affected as
well. For example, lower domestic prices may attract tourism from abroad
while private foreign investments, and thus long-term capital inflows,
may be discouraged by breaking down the protection wall. However these
phenomena are so difficult to quantify that they are usually ignored
with the estimation of exchange rate adjustments in the protection
context. By so doing it is implicitly assumed that the combined effect
of the elimination of the protection system and the exchange rate
adjustment upon the sum of the remaining entries in the real sphere is
zero, and consequently attention may be limited to the commodity
balance.

But if only the commodity balance is taken into account, there is
an-other problem that must be considered. Equilibrium on the balance of
payments in the sense described in the subsection 7.1.1. may be
perfectly compatible with surpluses or deficits on the commodity
balance. Thus if the balance of payments was in equilibrium in the
protection situation, the free-trade exchange rate is not the rate at
which the commodity balance would be in equilibrium but rather the one
which would bring the commodity balance back to the surplus or deficit
of the protection situation. If the balance of payments was not in
equilibrium in the protection situation - let us assume there was a

2. Most authors do this implicitly. See sections 2.4 and 2.5.

deficit DEF - then the free-trade exchange rate is the rate at which the commodity balance would achieve an improvement of DEF in comparison with the protection situation.

The latter case clearly demonstrates that in order to come to a proper estimation of the free-trade exchange rate, it is first necessary to define the surplus or deficit on the balance of payments in the protection situation. This complication is often avoided by redefining the free-trade exchange rate simply as the one that restores the existing (net) surplus of the commodity balance irrespective of whether the balance of payments itself was in equilibrium under protection.

Altogether the exchange rate adjustment in the protection context has a limited scope. It does not pretend to estimate equilibrium exchange rates for countries with high debt servicing ratios in varying international circumstances, nor anything of the kind. It does pretend to compensate the disruption of the commodity balance provoked by the elimination of the system of protection or, if the balance of payments was in disequilibrium in the protection situation, to correct also this disequilibrium through the commodity balance. Some of the consequences of these simplifications are spelt out in the following subsection.

7.1.3 Actual Devaluations and the Protection Concepts

Let us consider the not uncommon case of a country attempting to remedy a chronic deficit on the balance of payments with a restrictive import regime. The inflation records of the recent past suggest that the country's currency is notably overvalued, but adhering to a fixed exchange rate system the government is unwilling to come to an actual devaluation.

Looking at the situation from the protection point of view the government is doing two things. On the one hand it is providing positive protection to specific industries through the restrictive import regime and on the other it is giving a uniform negative protection to the economy as a whole[3] by maintaining an overvalued currency. The positive

---

3. It may be argued that this negative protection is not imposed on the economy as a whole but on the tradable goods only. This would be the case if only short-run effects were considered. In the long run it is assumed that after a transition period the prices of the non-tradables follow the trend of the tradeables. See also subsection 8.2.1.

protection is measured by the ordinary nominal and effective rates of protection, as described earlier, and the uniform negative protection is reflected by the exchange rate adjustment required to bring the balance of payments to equilibrium (not to the existing deficit!) in the free-trade situation. As long as the balance of payments remains in deficit in the protection situation, the negative protection derived from the overvaluation grossly outweighs the positive protection from the import regime and the net protective effect will be negative on the average, although specific industries may still receive positive protection.

After a while the unavoidable happens. The deficit can no longer be financed and external pressures force the government to a de-facto devaluation. Let us assume that the devaluation is of T.100 per cent, that is, the new exchange rate $r' = r (1+T)$. It is worth noting that although both the devaluation and the exchange rate adjustment to the free-trade situation aim at equilibrium on the balance of payments, they are not the same. The difference is that with the actual devaluation the system of protection is maintained, while with the exchange rate adjustment it is not.

Assuming that the devaluation causes domestic prices to go up by S.100 per cent on the average with S smaller than T, let us now consider the consequences for the ordinary and net rates of protection. As a result of the devaluation all unadjusted free-trade prices increase a uniform percentage of T.100 while protection prices increase only by S.100 per cent on the average. That is to say, average ordinary nominal (and thus also effective) protection decreases:

$$(7.1) \quad 1 + w'_{av} = \frac{1 + S}{1 + T} (1 + w_{av})$$

where w_{av} is the average ordinary nominal protection before the devaluation and w'_{av} after it. Thus, although the devaluation evidently raises the level of protection by making competition from abroad more expensive, the ordinary rates of protection decrease on the average. However contradictory this may seem it is a direct consequence of the way the ordinary rates of protection are defined.

Turning attention to the net rates of protection, it should be realised that the free-trade exchange rate $\overline{r}^{ft}$ does not depend on whether the system of protection is eliminated before or after the

actual devaluation. Consequently the exchange rate adjustment to free
trade before (ϕ) and after the devaluation (ϕ') are related in the
following way:

(7.2) $(1+\phi') = (1+\phi)/(1+T)$

Recalling the standard conversion (3.7) from ordinary to net nominal
rates, the relation between average net nominal protection before the
devaluation ($\overline{w}_{av}$) and after it ($\overline{w}'_{av}$) is:

(7.3) $(1+\overline{w}'_{av}) = \dfrac{1+w'_{av}}{1+\phi'} = \dfrac{1+S}{1+T} \cdot \dfrac{1+T}{1+\phi}\ (1+w_{av}) = (1+S)(1+\overline{w}_{av})$

Evidently the net protective rates measure the real protective effects
more adequately than the ordinary rates. The latter only reflect the
protective effect of the trade policy measures. The net rates add to
this effect the uniform negative protection resulting from the
overvalued exchange rate.

Summarising, it is seen that there are two kinds of overvaluation.
First there is a real overvaluation responsible for the deficit in the
presence of the system of protection, and secondly there is a
hypothetical overvaluation which corresponds to the hypothetical deficit
that would be added to the existing one, should the system of protection
be abolished. The exchange rate adjustment (ϕ) before the devaluation
corrects both hypothetical and real overvaluation. Assuming that the
actual devaluation T precisely eliminates the deficit of the existing
situation, the exchange rate adjustment ϕ' after the devaluation
corresponds with the hypothetical part.

Using this terminology, it may be concluded that, if net protection
is not based on an equilibrium free-trade exchange rate but on a rate
that restores the existing deficit, the exchange rate adjustment only
contains the hypothetical part of the overvaluation and net protection
fails to measure the negative protection due to the real overvaluation.

7.2   Methods to Estimate the Free-Trade Exchange Rate

7.2.1 General Remarks

Passing over a number of monetary-oriented models of exchange rate determination which are not suited for protection calculations, there are two ways that free-trade exchange rates can be estimated. The first derives from price elasticities of supply and demand and is therefore called the elasticity approach. The second is based upon the purchasing power of the currency and is called the purchasing-power approach.

The purchasing-power parity as an indicator of equilibrium exchange rates has been the subject of lively discussions.[4] It has even been denied any predictive power in that field. However until recently most of the discussion has been centred around intercountry and intertemporal parity rates, while the protection subject, which is essentially different, is hardly touched upon in the context. In this section a number of arguments are brought up in defence of a purchasing-power approach when used in the protection context. To pave the way for these, the elasticity and the purchasing-power approaches are first set out.

7.2.2 The Elasticity Approach

The elasticity approach was originally designed to estimate the trade-reducing effects of a tariff system. As such, it is described by Johnson in his article, 'The Theory of Effective Protection and Preferences'.[5] But once the trade-reducing effects of a protective system are assessed, it is only one step further to using it also to estimate exchange rate adjustments. The procedure is explained in most standard works on protection.[6]

4. Balassa (1964) is extremely critical of the purchasing-power parity doctrine. Balassa and Schydlowsky (1968) write in a disparaging tone about those who 'continue to believe that purchasing-power parities... approximate the free-trade equilibrium rate of exchange'. For the recent state of the debate see the symposium on purchasing-power parity, in Journal of International Economics, May 1978.
5. See Johnson (1969).
6. See for example Corden (1971), ch. 5; or Balassa et al. (1971), p. 326.

Its point of departure is the wellknown one-commodity partial-
equilibrium model with a supply and demand curve. All cross elasticities
in production and consumption are assumed away.[7] Moreover factor supply
and income effects derived from one commodity are not fed back into the
supply and demand conditions of other commodities. If, at the holding
price, supply falls short of demand, the product is imported; if it
exceeds demand, the excess supply is exported. International supply and
demand are supposed to be fully elastic.

For the sake of convenience, all supply and demand curves are
assumed linear, a simplification of relatively little importance in the
light of the huge uncertainties of the estimation of such curves. For an
imported product i, the suppression of nominal protection at a rate w_i
provokes an increase in imports ΔM_i which can be written as:

$$(7.4) \quad \Delta M_i = \Delta D_i - \Delta X_i = (\eta_i D_i + \varepsilon_i X_i) \frac{w_i}{1+w_i}$$

where X_i and D_i are domestic supply and demand at protection levels but
              valued at free-trade prices;
      ε_i and η_i are the corresponding price elasticities measured at the
              protection levels of the straight lines; and
      $w_i/(1+w_i)$ expresses the relative price decrease.

It is implicitly understood that a product that was imported in the
protection situation will also be imported and even to a larger extent
under free trade. However goods that were non-traded may become imported
under free trade. These cases are not accounted for by formula (7.4).
Generally the elasticity approach assumes the absence of trade character
changes.

In the presence of intermediate demand, total demand D can be
divided into a final and an intermediate part. Supply X can then be made
to respond to changes in the price of value-added (effective rate)
rather than to changes in the price of output (nominal rate), while
intermediate demand is then supposed to follow the output changes of the
using industries. Such a system was elaborated by Johnson.[8] However in
view of the enormous difficulties involved in the estimation of supply

7. See Corden (1971), p. 110.
8. See Johnson (1969).

elasticities on a sectorwise basis, such systems are just theoretical constructions with little hope of practical application.

For the same reason it is not surprising that as soon as it comes to practical applications formula (7.4), instead of being refined, is simplified even further to get rid of the supply elasticities:

$$(7.5) \quad \Delta M_i = n_i^M \, M_i w_i / (1 + w_1)$$

where n^M is the price elasticity of demand for imports which is defined as:

$$(7.6) \quad n_i^M = \varepsilon_i \frac{X_i}{M_i} + n_i \frac{D_i}{M_i}$$

Formula (7.5) is in principle a one-commodity equation, but for lack of detailed information on elasticities by commodity it is usually applied to all imports taken together.[9]

For an exported product j a similar expression can be derived about the change in exports ΔE_j following the suppresion of a subsidy at a rate w_j (or of an export tax equivalent at a rate $- w_j$):

$$(7.7) \quad \Delta E_j = - \varepsilon_j^E \, E_j w_j / (1 + w_j)$$

where the price elasticity of export supply is defined as:

$$(7.8) \quad \varepsilon_j^E = \varepsilon_j \frac{X_j}{E_j} + n_j \frac{D_j}{E_j}$$

and is measured again at the protection values of the straight line.

Formula (7.7) also applies to the case where the elasticity of international demand for the exported product is finite. In that case the export supply elasticity ε^E does not only depend on the domestic elasticities ε and n in the simple form given by formula (7.8), but also on the elasticity of world demand and on the country's share in the world market.[10]

If the exchange rate is adjusted, the elimination of the protective

9. In this way the elasticity approach was applied by Balassa. See Balassa et al. (1971), p. 326.
10. The corresponding formulas are elaborated in ibid., p. 330.

system   leads   to   relative   price   reductions $\bar{w}/(1+\bar{w})$ instead
of $w/(1+w)$. Assuming that the standard rule (3.7) may be used to express
net nominal rates $\bar{w}$ in ordinary rates w, the relative price reduction
can be written as:

$$(7.9) \qquad \frac{\bar{w}}{1 + \bar{w}} = \frac{w - \phi}{1 + w}$$

where ϕ expresses the exchange rate adjustment, that is
$\phi = \bar{r}/r - 1$. Formulas (7.5) and (7.7) can be adjusted accordingly.

The exchange rate adjustment which brings the commodity balance
back to its original situation must then satisfy the following equation:

$$(7.10) \qquad \Delta M - \Delta E = \Sigma_i \, \eta_i^M \, M_i \, \frac{w_i - \phi}{1 + w_i} + \Sigma_j \, \epsilon_j^E \, E_j \, \frac{w_j - \phi}{1 + w_j} = 0$$

This leads to a solution for the unknown adjustment ϕ which can be
written as:

$$(7.11) \qquad \phi = \frac{\Sigma_i \eta_i^M \, M_i \, \frac{w_i}{1 + w_i} + \Sigma_j \epsilon_j^E \, E_j \, \frac{w_i}{1 + w_j}}{\Sigma_i \eta_i^M \, M_i \, \frac{1}{1 + w_i} + \Sigma_j \epsilon_j^E \, E_j \, \frac{1}{1 + w_j}}$$

This expression for the exchange rate adjustment coincides with the one
obtained by Balassa.[11] There is no complete equivalence with the
expression given by Corden[12] but this is due to the fact that Corden
takes the free-trade situation as his point of departure.

Formulas (7.10) and (7.11) are applicable to the case where the
exchange rate is adjusted in such a way that the existing deficit
(surplus) on the commodity balance is maintained. It is perfectly
possible that in the protection situation such a deficit (surplus) was
compensated by a surplus (deficit) of equal magnitude on the remaining
transactions above the line so that the balance of payments was in
equilibrium. Assuming then that the elimination of the system of
protection combined with the exchange rate adjustment has no influence
upon the remaining transactions above the line, the adjustment (7.11)
brings the balance of payments back to its initial equilibrium.

11. Ibid., p. 328, formula (26).
12. See Corden (1971), p. 113, formula (5.1).

If on the other hand the balance of payment was in deficit
(surplus) in the existing situation, the exchange rate adjustment (7.11)
leads to a free-trade situation showing the deficit DEF of the
protection situation. Should the free-trade exchange rate be interpreted
as the rate at which all transactions above the line taken together are
balanced, the adjustment would have to be extended so as to correct also
for the deficit DEF. Under the same assumptions - that is, no influence
upon the remaining transactions - this can be achieved by including the
term DEF in the numerator of formula (7.11).[13]

It is interesting that formula (7.11) expresses the exchange rate
adjustment as a weighted average of the nominal rates of protection of
the individual goods. The weights are formed by the trade displacement
factors $n_i^M M_i$ and $\varepsilon_j^E E_j$ deflated with the corresponding nominal rates of
protection. As a result of the assumption that there are no trade
character changes, goods that are non-traded in the protection situation
remain so in the free-trade situation and do not figure in the weighted
sum.

7.2.3 The Purchasing-Power Approach

Although the origins of the purchasing-power parity theory have
been traced back to the beginning of the seventeenth century[14] it has
become associated with the name of Cassel who stated it in 1916 in terms
of a strict quantity theory of money. According to Cassel,[15] 'the rate
of exchange between two countries will be determined by the quotient
between the general level of prices in the two countries'. This is
usually called the absolute version of the purchasing-power parity
theory. Next to it there is a relative version stating that, starting
with a period when equilibrium rates prevail, changes in relative
purchasing power of the currencies involved determine the necessary
adjustments in exchange rates.

In order to test the hypothesis empirically, some further
specification is indispensable. What sort of price levels or price
indices are to be used to measure (changes in) purchasing power? Must it
be producer, wholesale or consumer price levels? Or perhaps GDP

13. See Balassa et al. (1971), p. 328, formula (26a).
14. See Kalamotousakis (1978).
15. See Cassel (1916).

deflators? Another question to be answered is whether to take price
levels covering all goods and services produced in the countries or only
those that are traded or tradable.

The relative version of the purchasing-power parity theory is
easier to test empirically than the absolute version. For the latter,
intercountry price comparisons are required, whereas the former can do
it with intertemporal price indices or GDP deflators which are currently
elaborated by national statistical offices. Notwithstanding the
considerable statistical effort involved in establishing intercountry
price comparisons, the absolute version of the theory has also been
tested many times.[16]

Irrespective of the kind of price indices used, the outcome of
these tests does not uniformly support the purchasing-power parity
hypothesis. On the contrary, for both the absolute and the relative
versions important discrepancies are reported between (changes in)
purchasing-power parities; and (changes in) exchange rates.There seems
to remain some intuitive understanding among international-trade
economists and monetarists in the sense that it would be difficult to
find any alternative independent indicator for exchange rate adjustments
that would do better than purchasing-power parities. Consequently, in
order to explain the reported departures from an all too strict
purchasing-power parity rule, attention has turned to the search for
disturbing factors which were already foreseen in the formulation of the
theory by Cassel.

One such explanation is found in the non-tradable goods and
services. Balassa, in his previously cited paper on the purchasing-power
parity doctrine[17], elaborates a two-commodity two-country model to show
how intercountry differences in the prices of services affect the
relation between purchasing-power parity and the exchange rate. There he
comes up with ample evidence for his suggestion that relative
productivity differences between countries and sectors would make the
non-tradable services more expensive in countries with higher per capita

16. See Balassa (1964); Frenkel (1978); and Kravis and Lipsey (1978)
    a.o.
17. See Balassa (1964).

incomes so that purchasing-power parities tend to overvalue the currencies of the poorer countries.[18]

Another factor which may cause exchange rates to deviate from purchasing-power parities is the system of protection. It is well known that on many occasions overvaluation of currencies is made possible by import-restrictive or export-promoting measures. In fact import restriction is often applied as a substitute for devaluation. For that reason one of the presumptions of the purchasing-power parity theory is that trade among the countries involved is relatively free. With that in mind it is surprising that, apart from some theoretical models,[19] few attempts have been made to quantify the role of the foreign-trade regime in the relation between purchasing-power parities and exchange rates empirically.

The most obvious way in which the upward pressure of foreign-trade regimes upon exchange rates can be quantified is by taking a weighted average of nominal or effective rates as a proxy for the strength of the regime. Then it can be assumed that the overvaluation of the currency permitted by the regime equals this average. By doing so it is easily verified that the absolute version of the purchasing-power parity theory holds by definition if the following conditions are met:

i. the average is drawn from nominal rates of protection which express price differences between domestic and international supply at the prevailing exchange rates;
ii. the countries involved face the same international supply prices;
iii. for both countries and for both purposes (protection and purchasing power) the same basket of goods is used.

Conditions (ii) and (iii) absorb all other disturbing factors such as transportation costs and trade directions (ii) and tastes and so on (iii). Condition (i) together with the hypothesis, accounts for the role

---

18. Balassa does not mention the possibility of measuring purchasing power in terms of the traded goods only. Should he have done so, the numerical example he chose would have been in complete support of the purchasing-power parity rule. Whether his empirical findings would also have supported the rule remains questionable, of course.
19. Such models can be found in Johnson (1966) and Eichengreen (1983) a.o.

of the system of protection. In fact it makes the system of protection responsible for any remaining departures from the purchasing-power parity rule.

For that reason the suggested quantification of the effect of the system of protection on the exchange rate does not prove the validity of the purchasing-power parity rule but rather makes it trivial. It remains as questionable as before whether indeed exchange rates react upon foreign-trade regimes the way it is assumed above.

Anyway the assumption provides a short-cut solution to the problem of defining the free-trade exchange rate. A second country is not needed, as the comparison of purchasing power can be performed direct between the protection and the free-trade situation. In the next subsection a proposition is offered of the choice of the basket and the assumption is fitted in an algebraic formulation.

7.2.4 Purchasing-Power Parity and Exchange Rate Adjustment

In the normal case where nominal protective rates are positive on the average, the elimination of the system of protection without a simultaneous adjustment of the exchange rate would lead to a situation in which the average price level is lower than in the protection situation. In other words the purchasing power of money under free-trade would be higher than under protection. Thus, even when protection increases the value-added of positively protected sectors, it remains to be seen if these sectors are really better off, given the fact that the goods and services on which this higher value-added is spent become more expensive as a result of the very same protection.

In the purchasing-power parity approach it is assumed that the exchange rate is adjusted in such a way that the purchasing power of the currency remains the same. By so doing, apart from the supposed restoration of equilibrium of the balance of payments, there is a further consequence that effective protection no longer measures the protection of value-added in money terms but in terms of purchasing power.

Here it is proposed to measure the purchasing power on the basket of domestic final demand including the non-tradable goods and services and imports for final demand. Following the notation of Chapter 5, the value at protection prices of the domestic-final-demand basket net of commodity taxes[20] is:

(7.12) $\iota_T \ DFD_T + \iota_N \ DFD_N + M_F + TI_F$

Assuming the standard relation (3.7) between ordinary and net nominal rates, the value of the same basket at the adjusted free-trade prices becomes:

(7.13) $(1 + \phi) \left\{ \iota_T \ (I + \hat{W}_T)^{-1} \ DFD_T + \iota_N \ (I + \hat{W}_N)^{-1} \ DFD_N + M_F \right\}$

By equating expressions (7.12) and (7.13), the following expression is obtained for the exchange rate adjustment ϕ:

(7.14) $\phi = \dfrac{W_T \ \hat{V}_T \ DFD_T + W_N \ \hat{V}_N \ DFD_N + W_M \ M_F}{\hat{V}_T \ DFD_T + \hat{V}_N \ DFD_N + M_F}$

As in the elasticity approach, the exchange rate adjustment is expressed as a weighted average of nominal rates. In the present approach, the weights are no longer the deflated trade displacement factors but the deflated values of the domestic-final-demand basket.

Expression (7.14) is obtained by equating the purchasing power of money in the protection situation with that under free trade. But in the protection situation should the balance of payments be in disequilibrium - say in a deficit of magnitude DEF - the reduction of purchasing power achieved by the adjustment ϕ according to (7.14) would not be sufficient to also eliminate the existing deficit. To that end it would be necessary to reduce the purchasing power of money further so as to reduce domestic final expenditures to an amount DEF. In the long run the latter effect may be incorporated by including a positive term DEF in the numerator of expression (7.14). The similarity with the elasticity approach is evident.

The effect of including the non-tradables in the purchasing power

---

20. As commodity taxes are supposed to persist on a specific basis under free trade, these taxes do not influence the relation discussed here.

basket greatly depends on what is assumed about the price response of
these goods and services to the elimination of the system of protection.
Evidently the assumptions regarding exchange rate adjustment on one hand
and price response of the non-tradables on the other are not
independent. The relation is discussed in more detail in section 8.2.

7.2.5 Elasticity versus Purchasing-Power Approach

As observed above, the purchasing-power parity theory has been
criticised severely. Balassa, after scrutinising the theory and testing
it empirically,[21] reaches a categorical rejection. For the purpose of
exchange rate adjustment in the protection context he advocates instead
the elasticity approach[22] and that is also the method he used in the
protection study for developing countries.[23] However he did not subject
the elasticity approach to an equally critical examination. But if he
had made such a test it would not be surprising if the result had been
equally unfavourable.[24]

It is not possible to review the whole discussion between
financiers and economists on the subject of trade imbalances and the
exchange rate. Both approaches have been tested, tests have been
criticised and, after all, it still seems to be rather a matter more of
belief than fact. In this subsection, only some arguments from the
protection point of view are added to the discussion.

Balassa, for example, in his criticism of the purchasing-power
parity hypothesis, argues that price differences in non-tradable
services may cause departures from both absolute and relative versions
of the purchasing-power parity rule. But his argument applies to
intercountry and intertemporal comparisons and not necessarily to the
'intersituation' comparisons required for protection calculations. In
fact if it were only for the differences in the prices of the non-
tradable services, the purchasing-power parity presumption would be only
one assumption away, namely that the prices of such services would be
the same in the protection and in the free-trade situation. The latter

21. See Balassa (1964).
22. See Balassa and Schydlowsky (1968).
23. See Balassa et al. (1971), App. A.
24. There is also the short-run versus long-run issue which makes the
    testing of the hypothesis ambiguous in both approaches. See also
    McKinnon (1980).

assumption seems much more reasonable than to assume that the relative
prices of these services would not change over a period or that they
would be the same between countries at different per-capita income
levels.

Likewise other factors, such as transport costs, differences in
tastes and so on, reflected by Cassel's K factor[25] may be responsible
for departures from an all too strictly interpreted purchasing-power
parity rule without invalidating a somewhat broader interpretation. As
such factors need not be constant over a period they provide the theory
with an escape from negative test results in both absolute and relative
versions. But also in this respect the purchasing-power parity rule is
likely to do better in the protection context as long as transport
costs, tastes, and so on differ less from the protection to the free-
trade situation than among countries and over a period.

There are two other arguments in support of the purchasing-power
approach. One is purely opportunistic; the other touches on the
interpretation of the net effective rate. The opportunistic argument is
that the purchasing-power parity adjustment is easier to calculate than
the elasticity adjustment. For the latter it is necessary to estimate
such tricky quantities as elasticities, while for the calculation of the
former no other information is required than the domestic-final-demand
flows of the already available input-output table and their nominal
protective rates.

The other argument is that the exchange rate adjustment based on
the purchasing-power principle leads to a net-effective-protection
concept which is meaningful in itself significant even when the
adjustment should fail to bring about equilibrium in the balance of
payments. To be more explicit, net effective protection calculated with
a purchasing-power type adjustment of the exchange rate compares the
purchasing power of value-added between the protection and the free-
trade situation rather than value-added in money terms. Such protection
of the purchasing power of value-added is a better indicator of the
protection given to the industries than any protection concept of value-
added in money terms that does not consider the prices of goods and
services on which it is spent, though with the latter concept the

25. See Niehans (1980).

balance of payments might be in disequilibrium. It must be admitted
however that if net protection is considered from this point of view,
the use of the term 'exchange rate adjustment' could be misleading, and
perhaps it would be better to rephrase it as 'purchasing-power
adjustment'.

8 Net protection

8.1 Net Effective Protection

8.1.1 Standard Conversion

The definition of nominal protection and the discussion of the concept in Chapter 3 are applicable irrespective of whether or not the exchange rate is adjusted to the free-trade situation. The same holds true for the definition of effective protection given in sections 5.1 and 5.2. However from the input-output calculations of section 5.3 onwards and throughout Chapter 6 it is assumed that the exchange rate of the protection situation persists under free trade. Here, this simplifying assumption is relaxed and the implications of exchange rate adjustment for the protection concepts are spelt out further.

In what follows, two free-trade situations are distinguished: one in which the exchange rate is not adjusted, to be called the unadjusted free-trade situation, and the other, the adjusted free-trade situation, in which the exchange rate is different from the one holding in the protection situation. Consequently there are also two sorts of free-trade prices: the adjusted ones and the unadjusted ones.

In normal circumstances, that is, under perfect competition, in the absence of trade character changes between one free-trade situation and the other and with all tradable goods traded in both free-trade situations, the adjusted free-trade prices of the tradables are 100 ϕ per cent higher than the unadjusted ones. Should there be trade character changes as a result of the adjustment or if certain tradable goods remain non-traded in any of the free-trade situations, the increase may be less. For the purpose of the argument such complications are assumed away.

If the prices of non-tradable inputs and the indirect taxes should go up by the same percentage, 100 ϕ, the value-added would also show the same increase, that is:

$$(8.1) \qquad \bar{y}^{ft} = (1+\phi)y^{ft}$$

where $\bar{y}^{ft}$ and y^{ft} stand for the value-added at adjusted and unadjusted free-trade prices respectively.

Recalling definition (5.1) of the effective rate of protection, relation (8.1) leads to the following standard relation between ordinary and net effective rates:

(8.2) $(1+\bar{z}) = (1+z)/(1+\phi)$

It is interesting to note that this relation has exactly the same shape as the standard relation (3.7) which converts ordinary nominal rates of protection into net ones.

As soon as trade character changes for the tradable goods are permitted, the standard conversion (3.7) for nominal protection does not hold any more. Moreover if the assumption of the price response of the non-tradables or that of the indirect domestic taxes is not in line with the supposedly uniform increase in the free-trade prices of the tradables, there is a further breakdown of relation (8.2).

In the remainder of this section, the way that net effective rates of protection can be calculated in such cases is set out. In fact the changes in the revaluation procedure provoked by the exchange rate adjustment are indicated and the departures from the standard conversion rule (8.2) are analysed. In section 8.2 the interdependence between the assumed price response of the non-tradables on one hand and the exchange rate adjustment on the other is dealt with: there too is found a reconsideration of the assumptions of indirect taxation under free trade. In section 8.3 the implications of an exchange rate adjustment for the economy-wide balancing of protection are spelt out.

8.1.2 Revaluation of the Input-Output Table Once Again

Roughly, the conversion of the valuation of the input-output table from existing to free-trade prices along the lines of the revaluation procedure discussed in subsection 5.3.3, remains valid if the following changes are carried through.

  i. All nominal rates of protection W along with the corresponding deflators V are substituted by net nominal rates $\bar{w}$ and adjusted deflators $\bar{V}$ according to formulas (3.8) or (3.9).
 ii. Assuming that export contracts are in foreign-currency terms the

export column is multiplied by a factor $(1+\phi)$.

iii. Also imports are supposed to keep their foreign-currency prices. Consequently their value at domestic prices must be multiplied by the same factor $(1+\phi)$. This occurs in step 3, formula (5.13) and in the adjustment of the value-added, formulas (5.15).

As a result of these changes the following expressions are obtained for the value-added at adjusted free-trade prices:

(8.3a) $\qquad \overline{Y}_T^{ft} = \overline{V}_T(\hat{X}_T - \hat{E}_T - \hat{A}_{TT}) - \overline{V}_N A_{NT} + (1+\phi)\ (E_T - M_T) - TD_T^{ft}$

(8.3b) $\qquad \overline{Y}_N^{ft} = \overline{V}_N\ (\hat{X}_N - \hat{E}_N - A_{NN}) - \overline{V}_T A_{TN} + (1+\phi)\ (E_N - M_N) - TD_N^{ft}$

The resulting input-output table at adjusted free-trade prices is obtained in the same way as that of Chapter 5. It resembles Table 5.2, but now the deflators carry a bar, the import row and the export column are multiplied by the factor $(1+\phi)$, the totals of rows and columns are adjusted and the value-added is obtained as a residue from the adjusted values according to equations (8.3a, b).

8.1.3 Departures from the Standard Rule

The standard conversion (8.2) from ordinary to net effective rates is based upon the presumption that the value added at adjusted free-trade prices is a factor $(1+\phi)$ higher than that at unadjusted free-trade prices. By comparing expressions (8.3) with the corresponding ones for the value added at unadjusted free-trade prices (5.15), it becomes possible to check the validity of this relation and to examine the sources of eventual discrepancies.

To that end, it is first understood that in the normal circumstances of subsection 8.1.1 the adjusted deflators for the tradables $\overline{V}_T$ are a factor $(1+\phi)$ higher than the unadjusted deflators V_T so that corresponding terms in equations (5.15) and (8.3) show the expected relation. Reversing the argument, abnormal circumstances - that is, trade character changes resulting from the adjustment or non-tradedness of tradables under free trade - are sources of departures from the standard rule. For simplicity it is assumed in the following that circumstances are normal in the above sense so that the tradable parts of equations (5.15) and (8.3) do not upset the standard relation.

The way in which the deflators for the non-tradables respond to the adjustment of the exchange rate does not depend on international prices, corrective terms or exchange rates but is defined by assumption. With that in mind, the assumptions regarding the adjusted and unadjusted free-trade prices of the non-tradables can be manipulated in such a way that the standard rule is not violated. How this can be achieved is discussed in the next section.

Finally a third source of disturbances of the standard relation is formed by the indirect-tax system. So far it has been assumed that the indirect-domestic-tax system remains in force in the free-trade situation on a specific basis irrespective of the exchange rate holding in the free-trade situation. A direct consequence of this assumption is that the indirect-tax terms of equations (8.3) in the adjusted free-trade situation are not a factor $(1+\phi)$ higher but equal to those of equations (5.15). Thus, here the standard rule is definitely violated unless different assumptions are made about the indirect-domestic-tax system under free trade. Such alternative assumptions are also discussed in the following section.

8.2   Exchange Rate Adjustment, Non-Tradables and Indirect Taxes

8.2.1 Price Response of the Non-Tradeables

First of all, the validity of the assumption of the price response of the non-tradables is not independent of that in respect of to the free-trade exchange rate. To make this clear, let us assume that a system of positive nominal protection is eliminated without adjusting the exchange rate. In the so-obtained free-trade situation, competition from abroad will force down the prices of the tradables. As a consequence the assumption of no price response whatsoever of the non-tradables (original Balassa method) places these latter goods in a position apart. Probably it would be more realistic to assume a uniform price decrease for the non-tradables, as is done in the Scott method, in order to re-establish the balance between the average price levels of tradables and non-tradables.

But the elimination of the system of protection is accompanied by an exchange rate adjustment, the downward price trend of the tradable goods is at least partly compensated by the adjustment. Whether, on balance, the price of a specific product declines or increases depends on its nominal rate of protection on the one hand and the magnitude of the adjustment on the other. If the latter should be larger than the nominal rate the price of the product would even increase. Thus if the exchange rate adjustment is assumed equal to the average level of nominal protection, the average price level of the tradable goods does not change with the transition to the adjusted free-trade situation. In such circumstances the assumption of the original Balassa method - no price response of the non-tradables - does not provoke the gap between tradables and non-tradables that it provokes in the absence of an exchange rate adjustment. For that reason, this assumption seems more realistic under exchange rate adjustment.

It should also be remembered that in this study the free-trade situation is not interpreted as the situation obtained directly after an abrupt elimination of the system of protection. Instead it is assumed that in the free-trade situation all short-term forces have run their course.[1] If in reality a system of protection with, on the average, positive nominal rates is eliminated without a concurrent adjustment of the exchange rate, the situation obtained directly afterwards will be characterised by a short-term imbalance between the average price levels of tradables and non-tradables. Whereas the prices of the tradables will be forced down by competition from abroad, the price level of the non-tradables is not exposed to such direct pressure.

There are two ways to restore the balance between tradables and non-tradables: the spontaneous way and the one of exchange rate adjustment. In the spontaneous way the price gap will cause demand to move away from non-tradables into tradables and supply in the opposite direction. Through that mechanism the downward pressure on the price level of the tradables is indirectly transferred to that of the non-tradables and in the long run the balance will be restored.[2]

However due to the rigidity of price levels, particularly their un-willingness to move downwards, it is preferable to adjust the exchange rate. By so doing, the gap between tradables and non-tradables is

1. See section 2.8.
2. A short-run transition model describing this phenomenon can be found in Connolly et al. (1976); and Dornbusch (1973).

avoided from the start and the adjustment process through production
factor movements, which may be costly, can be reduced to a minimum, even
though both ways should lead to essentially equivalent[3] situations in
the long run.

8.2.2 The Original Balassa Method under Exchange Rate Adjustment

In this method it is assumed that the prices of the non-tradables
in the adjusted free-trade situation are equal to their protection
prices, that is:

$$(8.4) \qquad \bar{W}_N = 0 \qquad\qquad or \qquad\qquad \bar{V}_N = \iota_N$$

Following the standard relation (3.7) between ordinary and net nominal
rates, it is easily verified that the assumption of equation (8.4) is
equivalent to the assumption of a uniform ordinary rate for all non-
tradables equal to the magnitude of the exchange rate adjustment:

$$(8.5) \qquad W_N = \phi\iota_N \qquad\qquad or \qquad\qquad V_N = (1+\phi)\iota_N$$

This latter assumption coincides exactly with that of the original Scott
method provided that the exchange rate adjustment ϕ is chosen equal to
the average nominal protection of the tradables according to formula
(6.10).

It can be proved that the exchange rate adjustment obtained with
the purchasing-power approach according to equation (7.14) is indeed
equal to the average nominal protection of the tradables according to
expression (6.10). To that end it is sufficient to substitute formula
(8.5) in the right-hand side of equation (7.14) and solve the exchange
rate adjustment ϕ as the unknown variable.

The equivalence between the assumption of the original Scott method
without exchange rate adjustment and that of the original Balassa method
with an adjustment calculated as described above can be made explicit by
comparing the input-output tables at free-trade prices obtained with one
method and then the other. Following again the standard conversion (3.7)

---

3. Under homogeneous supply and demand functions, the situations would
   only differ by a numerary ratio for the prices of goods, production
   factors and foreign exchange.

for nominal protection on which equation (7.14) is based, the exchange rate adjustment itself raises all tradable flows of the table - including the import row and export column - by a factor $(1+\phi)$. On the other hand the special way of choosing the assumptions concerning the price response of the non-tradables establishes the same relation between the non-tradable flows of the tables.

Altogether the whole upper part - that is, the first and second quadrants plus the import row - of the input-output table at free-trade prices obtained with the original Balassa method with adjustment, is a factor $(1+\phi)$ higher than that of the corresponding table obtained with the original Scott method without adjustment. Owing to the identity between row and column totals in input-output tables, the same multiplicative relation extends to the column totals of the first and third quadrants.

Turning now to the columns, the only flows left are those of indirect taxes and value-added. If these flows were aggregated to a single one, the aggregated flows[4] would necessarily show the same multiplicative relation because they are obtained as residues. This does not imply that the same holds true for the indirect-tax and value-added flows taken separately. On the contrary, if the assumption of the indirect-tax system under free trade is not changed along with the exchange rate adjustment the indirect-tax flows do not vary from one case to the other, so that the increase by a factor $(1+\phi)$ of the aggregate flows are there on account of the value-added components only. Therefore the factor relating the value-added at adjusted free-trade prices to that at unadjusted free-trade prices will be somewhat higher than $(1+\phi)$, at least if the indirect-tax component is positive.

In view of the fact that the indirect-tax flows are normally small in comparison with the value-added terms, the resulting departures from the standard conversion (8.2) for effective protection will also be small. In the next subsection it is demonstrated that with a minor modification of the assumption of the indirect-tax system under free trade, the correspondence by a uniform factor $(1+\phi)$ can be extended to

---

4. It may be tempting to conclude that the aggregate flows stand for value-added at market prices. However, as the fact that the indirect-tax flows represent taxes on inputs rather than on output, such an interpretation would be mistaken.

all flows of the input-output table, which makes the equivalence between
the original Balassa method with adjustment and the original Scott
method without adjustment complete.

8.2.3 The Indirect-Tax System under Free Trade

So far it has been assumed that under free trade indirect domestic
taxes remain in force on a specific basis, that is, the amount of taxes
payable depends on volumes not on values. Thus if the value of a
specific flow changes as a result of the transition from protection to
free-trade prices the amount of indirect commodity taxes to be paid
remains unchanged. As far as non-commodity taxes are concerned, these
are also assumed to remain unaffected as long as the output of the
paying sectors does not change.

Alternatively it can be assumed that indirect domestic taxes remain
in force on an ad-valorem basis. In that case, indirect commodity taxes
are assumed to vary proportionally with the value of the corresponding
flows and non-commodity taxes with the value of production of the paying
sectors. If, for example, the price of a certain product decreases on
the elimination of the protective system, this assumption implies that
the corresponding indirect taxes decrease in the same proportion. In
this subsection the implications for the revaluation procedure of
section 5.3 are briefly set out.

First, the assumption of the indirect-tax system adopted in Chapter
2 has had certain consequences for the way the input-output flows are
deflated in Chapter 5. As nominal rates of protection are defined in
terms of basic prices - that is, excluding indirect commodity taxes - a
conversion of the valuation of the input-output table from producers'
prices to basic prices is necessary before starting the revaluation
procedure. If alternatively it is assumed that indirect taxes vary
proportionally with the value of the flows, no such conversion is necessary because the deflation is equally applicable to the commodity-tax
part of the flows.

As a consequence, with the indirect-domestic-tax system on an ad-
valorem basis the revaluation procedure of Chapter 5 can begin with the
input-output table valued at producers' prices. In such a registration
the row for indirect commodity taxes refers to taxes on the output of
the corresponding sector (rather than on inputs) and has no entries in

the fourth quadrant. It is easily verified that the only formula to be
adapted is formula (5.14a) which describes indirect domestic taxes under
free trade. As both components (commodity and non-commodity) are now
related to the value of output, they should be deflated with the same
deflators as output itself. that is:

$$(8.6) \qquad TD_J^{ft} = TD_J(I+\hat{W}_J)^{-1} = TD_J\hat{V}_J \qquad (J = T,N)$$

As the indirect-tax row has no entries in the fourth quadrant, the
superscipt J only takes the values T and N.

With only a few minor changes which are all straightforward, the
input-output calculations of effective protection presented in Chapters
5 and 6 remain applicable. The only substantial changes are found in the
modified Balassa and Scott methods. In these methods the term TD_N of
equations (6.4) and (6.13) must be replaced by $TD_N\hat{V}_N$ which makes them
dependent on the unknown deflators V^N so that the solution of the system
is affected. Similar changes can be carried through in the modified
Corden method.

Turning back to the comparison between the original Scott method
without and the original Balassa method with exchange rate adjustment,
it becomes apparent that, with the new assumptions (8.6) about indirect
taxes under free trade, the multiplicative relation by a factor $(1+\phi)$ is
automatically transferred to the indirect-tax row and is thus also
enforced upon value-added obtained as a residue. Consequently the
equivalence between the original Scott method without exchange rate
adjustment and the original Balassa method with an adjustment according
to equation (7.14) becomes complete once the indirect-domestic-tax
system is assumed to persist on an ad-valorem basis.

A similar equivalence can be proved to exist between the modified
Scott method without and the modified Balassa method with exchange rate
adjustment. To that end, the exchange rate adjustment must be defined in
terms of GDP deflators rather than in terms of price indices on domestic
final demand. However the proof of the equivalence would lead us too far
away and is left as an exercise for the reader.

8.3   Average Net Protection

8.3.1 Exchange Rate Adjustment and Average Protection

Following again the standard conversion for nominal and effective protection, a positive exchange rate adjustment ϕ lowers all protective rates in the uniform way described by formulas (3.7) and (8.2). If an ordinary rate happens to be equal to the adjustment ϕ, the corresponding net rate results zero. For that reason, if the exchange rate adjustment is chosen equal to a weighted average of ordinary rates, the weighted average of the net rates is expected to be about zero.

In both the elasticity and the purchasing-power approach, the exchange rate adjustment can be expressed as a weighted average of nominal protective rates provided that the balance of payments is in equilibrium[5] in the protection situation. In the elasticity approach the weights are the trade displacement factors of formula (7.11). In the purchasing-power approach the weights are the domestic-final-demand flows valued at free-trade prices.

In the remainder of this chapter an exchange rate adjustment according to formula (7.14), which corresponds with the purchasing-power approach, is assumed. With such exchange rate adjustment, it is easily verified that average net nominal protection on the domestic-final-demand basket is zero. In section 5.4, however, average nominal protection on domestic final demand is shown to be equal to average effective protection on value-added. Consequently average net effective protection must necessarily be zero too. In the following subsections this is demonstrated independently of the assumption in respect of the price response of the non-tradables.

Finally it is worth noting that, with an exchange rate adjustment according to the elasticity approach, it is also possible to find vanishing weighted averages for net nominal and effective protection. However the weights required to achieve this do not have the intuitive significance they have in the other approach. Therefore they are not worked out further.

---

5. If the balance of payment is not in equilibrium, the net deficit term is added to the numerator of the average. See section 7.2.

8.3.2 Average Net Nominal Protection

The exchange rate is assumed to be adjusted according to the purchasing-power approach (7.14). Moreover the standard conversion (3.7) from ordinary to net rates is assumed to apply to all goods and services irrespectively whether they are tradable or non-tradable, domestically produced or imported. For the non-tradables this implies the rephrasing indicated above of the assumption, along with the adjustment of the exchange rate.

Average net nominal protection on domestic final demand can then be written as follows:

$$(8.7) \qquad \bar{w}_{av} = \frac{\bar{W}_T \; \overline{DFD}_T^{ft} + \bar{W}_N \; \overline{DFD}_N^{ft} + \bar{W}_M (1+\phi) M_F}{\iota_T \; \overline{DFD}_T^{ft} + \iota_N \; \overline{DFD}_N^{ft} + (1+\phi) M_F}$$

where the bars over the symbols refer to their valuation at adjusted free-trade prices. Recalling that domestic-final-demand flows at adjusted free-trade prices are a factor $(1+\phi)$ higher than the corresponding flows valued at unadjusted free-trade prices $(\overline{DFD}^{ft} = (1+\phi) \; DFD^{ft})$ the weights of formula (8.7) may be reduced to unadjusted free-trade valuation:

$$(8.8) \qquad \bar{w}_{av} = \frac{\bar{W}_T DFD_T^{ft} + \bar{W}_N DFD_N^{ft} + \bar{W}_M M_F}{\iota_T DFD_T^{ft} + \iota_N DFD_N^{ft} + M_F}$$

That is, it does not matter whether domestic final demand is valued at adjusted or unadjusted free-trade prices, as one is proportional to the other.

Applying the standard conversion (3.7) for nominal rates and substituting expression (7.14) for the exchange rate adjustment ϕ, it can easily be verified that the right-hand side of equation (8.8) reduces to zero:

$$(8.9) \qquad \bar{w}_{av} = 0$$

That is, average net nominal protection on domestic final demand disappears.

8.3.3 Average Net Effective Protection

To show that a similar relation holds for effective protection, let us turn to the input-output tables valued at existing protection prices (Table 5.1) and at adjusted free-trade prices (Table 5.2 adjusted according to subsection 8.1.2). In both tables the sum of the flows contained in the second quadrant must be equal to the sum of the flows in the third. Adding the complete fourth quadrant on both sides, the following equations are obtained:

$$(8.10) \qquad Y_{TOT} + IT_{TOT} + M_{TOT} = E_{TOT} + DFD_{TOT}$$

$$(8.11) \qquad \overline{Y}_{TOT}^{ft} + \overline{IT}_{TOT}^{ft} + (1+\phi)M_{TOT} = (1+\phi)E_{TOT} + \overline{DFD}_{TOT}^{ft}$$

Subtracting equation (8.11) from (8.10) and bringing the export terms to the left-hand side obtains the following equation:

$$(8.12)(Y_{TOT} - \overline{Y}_{TOT}^{ft}) + (IT_{TOT} - \overline{IT}_{TOT}^{ft}) - \phi(M_{TOT} - E_{TOT}) = DFD_{TOT} - \overline{DFD}_{TOT}^{ft}$$

Assuming again that the value added generated by the government remains the same in the adjusted free-trade situation, the right-hand side of equation (8.12) can be written as:

$$(8.13) \qquad DFD_{TOT} - \overline{DFD}_{TOT}^{ft} =$$

$$= \iota_T(DFD_T - \overline{DFD}_T^{ft}) + \iota_N(DFD_N - \overline{DFD}_N^{ft}) + (IT_F - \overline{IT}_F^{ft}) - \phi M_F =$$

$$= \overline{W}_T \overline{DFD}_T^{ft} + \overline{W}_N \overline{DFD}_N^{ft} + \overline{W}_M(1+\phi)M_F = 0$$

which vanishes as shown in subsection 8.3.2.

As a consequence the left-hand side of equation (8.12) must also be equal to zero. Following the explanation of subsection 5.4.1, this left-hand side can be interpreted in the following way.

The first term, that is, the difference between value-added at protection prices and at adjusted free-trade prices, represents total effective protection in absolute terms granted to the productive sectors. Remember that the value-added generated by the government Y_G, which is also contained in the total, is assumed to remain unaffected.

The second term stands for the difference in indirect-tax revenue between the protection situation and the adjusted free-trade situation. Along these lines it can be interpreted as the effective protection in absolute terms granted to the tax collector.

The third term refers to the balance of trade and represents the extra amount of national currency required to cover a deficit ($M^{TOT} - E^{TOT}$) at the adjusted exchange rate. It carries a minus sign because it implies a negative protection to the banks, which by selling the same amount of foreign exchange receive less national currency in the protection situation than they would have received under the adjusted exchange rate.

Thus the disappearance of the left-hand side of equation (8.12) implies that total effective protection, which can be split up in the above elements, is equal to zero. In equation (8.12) effective protection is stated in absolute terms. Stating it in relative terms, the left-hand side of (8.12) reads as the numerator of a weighted average and average effective protection also disappears.

As average net effective protection equals zero, individual net effective rates obtained with a purchasing-power exchange rate adjustment can be interpreted as the extent to which effective protection of the specific sector exceeds the average of the economy as a whole.

8.3.4 The Closed Circuit

In section 5.4 it is demonstrated that the changes in the prices of goods and services caused by the protective system provoke money transfers between producers, consumers and the government which in the end add up to zero. Total effective protection of the productive sectors and the government equals total negative protection of the purchasers of domestic final demand.[6] As the income of these purchasers ultimately comes from the value-added generated by the productive sectors and by the government, this system of transfers forms a closed circuit. That is, there are neither leakages nor net gains in the system.

By adjusting the exchange rate to the free-trade situation, as

6. See equation (5.19).

assumed here, this circuit of money transfers is split up into two
separate circuits, each of them closed. One of them is the nominal
protection circuit: that is the circuit of money transfers among the
purchasers of the domestic-final-demand basket. As average nominal
protection on domestic final demand is equal to zero, this circuit is
closed.

The other is the effective protection circuit. Apart from
protection of value-added of the productive sectors, this circuit
comprises protection of the tax collector through the indirect-tax
system and negative protection of the banking system resulting from the
(hypothetical) overvaluation of the exchange rate. The fact that the
total protection derived from these three elements equals zero implies
that the effective protection circuit is also closed.

9 The structure of protection in Mexico in 1980

9.1.1 Background to Protection in Mexico

Although protectionist measures, mostly in the form of import tariffs, have a long history in Mexico, until the Second World War they were of an individual nature. Only after the war, when competition from abroad regained its former strength, did a more comprehensive system of protection come into being, mainly to give the newly emerging manufacturing industry a chance.

During the fifties the principal aim of Mexican foreign-trade policies was to substitute imports of final-consumption goods. After a reasonably successful initial period the possibilities for a continued substitution of those goods were virtually exhausted and during the sixties attention gradually turned to the substitution of intermediate manufactures. In this way it was hoped to come to a further vertical integration of the domestic industrial sector.

Parallel to this development there has been an important effort to prevent the exportation of unprocessed raw materials. By imposing moderate taxes on the exportation of unprocessed agricultural and mineral products, the processing of these materials within the country was stimulated without affecting the competitive position of the processed materials in the international markets.

In 1970 these policies had led to a situation characterised by a slightly negative protection of the primary activities, a moderate positive protection of the intermediate manufactures and a considerable to strong protection of the consumer durables. To guarantee popular subsistence many non-durable consumption goods were kept cheap and the same holds true for most capital goods in order not to damage industrial and infrastructural investment.

The structure of protection so described is typical for developing countries aiming at industrialisation through import substitution. It is emphasised however that in Mexico this structure was less marked than in many other developing countries.The proximity of the United States and the threat of smuggling along a 3000-kilometre border limited Mexican potentialities to increase the levels of industrial protection further.

During the seventies foreign-trade policies became more and more dictated by balance of payments considerations. Although the basic protectionist structure did not change, import policies were tightened under the Echeverría administration in an attempt to control the growing external deficits which ultimately led to the 1976 devaluation. Afterwards they were released again by the huge oil revenues and the enormous capital inflows of the late seventies.

In 1981 when oil prices started to decline, and with an astronomical foreign debt, the Mexican government again resorted to foreign-trade measures, rather than restrictive monetary policies and a contraction of government spending, to face the forthcoming balance of payments deficits. As in the mid-seventies however such measures could not avoid the successive devaluations of the Mexican peso during 1982, after which the country was plunged into its worst recession of the last fifty years.

9.1.2 Quantitative Studies on Protection in Mexico

With the foreign-trade policy at the mercy of the balance of payments deficits, the levels of nominal and effective protection must have fluctuated heavily. However until recently it has not been possible to quantify these fluctuations systematically as only a few quantitative studies on protection in Mexico were available.

The first economy-wide measurement of nominal and effective protection was performed by Bueno.[1] The results of his study, which formed part of the intercountry study on the structure of protection sponsored by the World Bank, cover nominal and effective rates of protection for 35 sectors producing tradable goods for the year 1960.

A second comprehensive study on protection in Mexico was carried out by Ten Kate in cooperation with the Faculty of Economics of the National Autonomous University of Mexico.[2] Nominal and effective

1. The results were first published in the Mexican journal, Demografí y Economía. See Bueno (1972). An English version is in Balassa et al. (1971), ch. 8.
2. Nominal-protection estimates were presented by Waarts et al. (1976); effec-tive-protection estimates can be found in Ten Kate et al. (1977). For the results in English see Ten Kate et al. (1980), ch.2.

protection were quantified for 1970 in the same 35 sectors.

In 1979 the Mexican Ministry of Commerce felt the need to update these estimates to more recent years and made provisions to measure several indicators of protection, together with those of other industrial-incentive policies, on a regular basis. In July 1980 a pilot project started and a year later nominal and effective-protection estimates were completed for 59 sectors producing tradables for the year 1979. In the course of 1982 similar estimates for 1980 became available.

In section 9.2 protection estimates for 1980 are presented, which are closely related to the results of the latter study.[3] The nominal-protection estimates are taken direct. The effective rates are calculated under slightly different assumptions of indirect taxation under free trade. Moreover economic activities are aggregated to 24 sectors only.

The methodology adopted in the Ministry of Commerce study coincides roughly with the system elaborated here, so the results may be said to test its quality. Meanwhile some observations about trade and price policies around 1980 would be in order.

9.1.3 Trade and Price Policies around 1980

With inflation gradually increasing from 16 per cent per year in 1978 to almost 30 per cent in 1980 - which was then considered high - Mexican price policies were mainly of an anti-inflationary nature. By keeping the prices of a large number of foodstuffs and other popular non-durable consumption goods at a low level, the government intended to guarantee the subsistence of the poorer part of the population and at the same time break the inflationary spiral on that side. Under these policies price increases for a growing number of articles - in 1980 about 3000 - became subject to previous authorisation by the Ministry of Commerce.

As a result many of the controlled items remained cheap and the price gap between controlled and uncontrolled items increased steadily. In these circumstances the production of the controlled articles became less and less attractive, which often led to 'producers' strikes' attempting to force the Ministry of Commerce to authorise price increases

3. The results of this study have not yet been published but were made available to the Mexican government in the form of internal reports.

for the articles concerned. In order to break such producers' strikes,
the Ministry of Commerce often permitted temporary importation of those
products, at least when supply from abroad was still competitive at the
defended prices.

For a number of basic subsistence crops, wheat, beans and rice,
among others, import prices were well above controlled domestic
prices.To guarantee sufficient domestic supply at the controlled prices
huge quantities were imported by the state-administered company CONASUPO
and the gap between import and domestic distribution prices had to be
covered by enormous government subsidies.

Official pricing policies were also predominant in the energy
sector. One of the ways in which the Mexican government attempted to
make oil resources benefit national economic development was by making
energy available at prices far below those ruling in international
markets. Clearly such pricing policies had to be complemented by
measures in the foreign-trade sphere, such as export regulations to
prevent the cheap fuels being exported direct, and import subsidies in
case of insufficient domestic supply, as for most basic petrochemicals.

Foreign-trade policies were fairly liberal in the late seventies.
The enormous oil revenues together with important capital inflows made
foreign exchange so abundant that the traditionally restrictive import
policies could be loosened at an almost stable exchange rate without
provoking a foreign-exchange crisis. Strong voices from within the
government advocated Mexico's membership of the GATT and, anticipating
such a membership, a start was made with the liberalisation of the
foreign-trade regime, that is, with the substitution of licences by
equivalent tariffs.

The above measures led to a strongly negative nominal protection of
petroleum-derived products, a negative to slightly positive protection
of most of the goods subject to some form of price control and a
somewhat stronger but not extremely positive protection for the majority
of the uncontrolled articles. In 1979 the negative protection of the
petroleum-derived products and of some basic subsistence crops still
counterbalanced the positive protection of the other goods so that the
average nominal protection of the tradable part of the economy was about
zero.

In 1980 some important policy changes were carried out. At the beginning of the year the Mexican government decided not to become a member of the GATT and the gradual liberalisation of the foreign-trade regime became subject to severe criticism. Apart from that, the ever increasing deficits on both internal and external balances of the country required counteractive measures. In order to reduce the price support subsidies to subsistence crops, the controlled prices were increased considerably, but that did not prevent total government subsidies reaching the unprecedented level of 80 billion pesos in 1980. At the same time the increasing deficit on current account caused the government to tighten the foreign-trade regime again after a period of stepwise liberalisation.

However with an expansionary public spending programme and an internal inflation grossly outweighing that of its principal trade partner, the United States, the relatively smooth policy adjustments were insufficient by far to turn the tide. The deficits on the internal and external balances increased further, Mexico's competitive position in international markets became weaker, exports of manufactured goods declined and foreign-exchange earnings came to depend almost exclusively on crude oil.

When in the summer of 1981 oil prices started to decline in the international markets, a foreign-exchange crisis became unavoidable. In an attempt to remedy the situation the policy adjustments initiated in 1980 were intensified but the inertia of the economic system was too great. Existing reserves permitted postponing the crisis until February 1982 when the first of a number of successive devaluations of the Mexican peso had to be conceded.

The year for which the structure of protection is presented in the following sections is 1980. It marks the culmination of a period of extremely rapid expansion. The signals foreboding the coming crisis were still weak and the policy adjustments carried out did not affect the structure of protection in a drastic manner, although the average level of protection had increased from zero in 1979 to almost 10 per cent in 1980.

9.2   Nominal Protection

9.2.1 Sector Classification
In the project of the Ministry of Commerce, the economic activity classification of the national accounts statistics was followed.[4] In this classification 72 branches are distinguished, 59 of which produce tradable goods. For the purpose of the presentation given here, these 72 branches are aggregated to 24 sectors, and of these 19 sectors produce tradable goods while the remainder are considered to produce non-tradables.

A description of the aggregate sectors and their relation with the branches of national accounts is given in Table 9.1. The aggregation is performed in such a way that nominal protection does not vary too much between different branches contained in an aggregate sector. Nevertheless the intra-sector variation of nominal protection results large but this is mainly due to the fact that the variation within the branches was already strong. See also subsection 9.2.3 below.

9.2.2 The Sample
The sample of products for which nominal protection was measured consisted of 342 products. For 246 out of these nominal protection was defined by some sort of price comparison. For the remaining 96 products the filter for price comparisons, which is explained in section 4.3, interfered in one way or another in measuring the nominal rate of protection.

Out of the 246 price comparisons, 116 products had a reasonable degree of priceability. For 84 products unit value comparisons were necessary, while the nominal protective rates for the remaining 44 products were defined by identifying for each of them a number of products at the priceable level. The total number of subproducts covering these 44 products was 164, almost all of them in the motor-car sector.

4. National accounts for 1970 to 1978, published by the Secretaría de Programación y Presupuesto (1981). For the following years – 1979 and 1980 – see Secretaría de Programación y Presupuesto (1982).

Table 9.1 Economic Activity Classification

Aggregate Sectors	Corresponding National Account Branches
1. Agriculture	1 to 4
2. Energy Mining	5, 6
3. Other Mining	7 to 10
4. Meat and Dairy Products	11
5. Grain Milling and Products	13, 14
6. Vegetable Oils and Animal Feed	17, 18
7. Other Foodstuffs	12, 15, 16, 19
8. Beverages and Tobacco	20 to 23
9. Textile and Leather Products	24 to 28
10. Wood and Paper Products	29 to 32
11. Petroleum Products	33, 34, 36
12. Chemical Industries	35, 37 to 40
13. Rubber and Plastic Products	41, 42
14. Non-Metallic Mineral Products	43 to 45
15. Basic Metal Industries	46, 47
16. Metal Products including Machinery	48 to 52
17. Electric and Electronic Apparatus	53 to 55
18. Transport Equipment	56 to 58
19. Other Manufacturing Industries	59
20. Construction	60
21. Electricity	61
22. Commerce	62
23. Transport	64
24. Other Services	63, 65 to 72

Active filter interference does not necessarily imply that the price comparisons were not relevant in those cases. Only with strongly imported or exported products whose trade was not subject to quantitative restrictions, was the assignment of a nominal rate of protection direct, that is, irrespective of the price relations detected. That was so for 48 out of 96 products. In 43 cases the price comparison was relevant either to permit the product to enter the sample or to define whether the upper or lower limit of the interval should be taken. Finally for 5 products the nominal rate of protection was assumed to be zero because of doubtful tradability, as in the case of sugar cane, cow's milk, limestone, and others.

The intersector composition of the sample is given in Table 9.2. It should be noted that the distribution of products over sectors has little homogenity. Some sectors are covered by many products (agriculture by 60), others by only a few (grain milling by 3). A low number of products in a sector does not always mean a low representativeness of the sample. To give an example, the 4 products in energy mining (crude oil, natural gas, coque and graphite) cover well over 90 per cent of the production value of the sector. Generally however if the number of products (subproducts) is smaller than 10, the margin of error of the resulting nominal rate of protection becomes considerable. In such cases the information of the sample was complemented by information from other sources[5] to avoid nominal protection estimates being too far off the mark. There is a sector (19,other manufacturing industries) without any product in the sample. The nominal protective rate of this sector is calculated from the corresponding rate for 1979 and price indices applying on both domestic and free-trade prices.

5. Such other sources were: (i) direct consultations with
   representatives of the Ministry of Industrial Promotion and the
   private sector and (ii) price relations for other years, mainly
   1979, complemented with price indices.

Table 9.2 Sample Composition

	Price Comparisons		Filter Interference				
	Priceable Products	Non-Priceable Sub-products*	Unit-Values	Direct	In-direct	Hardly Tradable	Total
1. Agricult	25	–	6	21	5	3	60
2. Enerming	3	–	–	–	1	–	4
3. Othermin	7	–	–	4	5	2	18
4. Meatdair	6	–	7	–	1	–	14
5. Grainmil	3	–	–	–	–	–	3
6. Oilsfeed	9	–	3	–	–	–	12
7. Othfoods	6	1 (2)	4	2	4	–	17
8. Bevtobac	–	–	3	1	–	–	4
9. Textleat	2	1 (5)	9	1	6	–	19
10. Woodpape	5	–	6	2	2	–	15
11. Petropro	27	–	5	–	–	–	32
12. Cheminds	17	–	10	6	7	–	40
13. Rubplast	–	–	3	2	1	–	6
14. Nomminpr	2	–	5	3	1	–	11
15. Basmetal	4	–	11	5	5	–	25
16. Metprods	–	1 (2)	4	1	2	–	8
17. Electrap	–	–	9	–	3	–	12
18. Transpeq	–	41 (155)	1	–	–	–	42
19. Otherman	–	–	–	–	–	–	–
Total	116	44 (164)	86	48	43	5	342

* The figures of this column represent the number of products. Within parentheses, the number of constituent subproducts is indicated.

9.2.3 The Structure of Nomimal Protection

Nominal rates of protection are presented in Table 9.3. These rates refer to sales in the domestic market valued at basic prices. To give an impression of the dispersion of nominal protection between different products within a sector, the intrasector standard deviation and variance are also given.

Table 9.3 Nominal Protective Rates by Sector in Mexico in 1980

Aggregate Sectors	Nominal Protective Rate	Standard Deviation	Intra-Sector Variance*	Intra-Branch Variance**	Intra-B.to Intra-Sect. Variance
1. Agricult	10%	22%	.0490	.0474	97%
2. Enerming	-83%	8%	.0060	.0003	5%
3. Othermin	-4%	24%	.0578	.0087	15%
4. Meatdair	21%	36%	.1310	.1310	100%
5. Grainmil	-16%	10%	.0107	.0017	16%
6. Oilsfeed	10%	17%	.0301	.0259	86%
7. Othfoods	0%	20%	.0398	.0147	37%
8. Bevtobac	-18%	26%	.0658	-	-
9. Textleat	20%	17%	.0278	.0086	31%
10. Woodpape	19%	17%	.0274	.0109	40%
11. Petropro	-71%	19%	.0370	.0201	54%
12. Cheminds	21%	22%	.0488	.0368	75%
13. Rubplast	56%	17%	.0296	.0124	42%
14. Nomminp	7%	16%	.0247	.0225	91%
15. Basmetal	6%	10%	.0103	.0086	83%
16. Metprods	27%	16%	.0261	.0229	88%
17. Electrap	64%	46%	.2092	.1780	85%
18. Transpeq	39%	33%	.1078	.0656	61%
19. Otherman	35%	-	-	-	-

* The intra-sector variance can be decomposed into inter-branch variance and the sum of intra-branch variances. The decomposition is as follows:

$$isv = \Sigma_k X_k^{ft}(w_k^{av} - w_{sec}^{av})^2/\Sigma_k X_k^{ft} + \Sigma_k X_k^{ft} ibv_k/\Sigma_k X_k^{ft} \quad (k=\text{branches in sector})$$

$$= (\text{inter-branch variance}) + (\text{intra-branch variances})$$

** The intra-branch variance for branch k is defined as:

$$ibv_k = \Sigma_j X_j^{ft}(w_j - w_k^{av})^2/\Sigma_j X_j^{ft} \quad (j=\text{products in branch})$$

From Table 9.3 it becomes clear that the most negatively protected sectors are energy mining (2) and petroleum products (11). By far the most important product in energy mining is crude oil. As this product is either processed by the state-owned oil giant PEMEX or directly exported by the same company, there is no domestic market for crude oil and thus no domestic price.

However, for purposes of national accounting and in the input-output table, an internal accounting price is used to value the flow of crude oil from the extraction branch (in sector 2) to the refinery branch (in sector 11). This internal accounting price was set against the export price of crude oil of a similar API grade corrected for transport margins, to arrive at a nominal protective rate of -84 per cent. Other negatively protected products are found in the sectors: other mining, grain milling and beverages and tobacco products. Most sectors with a moderate positive nominal protection (between 0 and 25 per cent) produce intermediate manufactures and non-durable consumption goods. Only in sectors 9 and 10 is there some production of consumption durables (apparel and shoes in sector 9 and books in sector 10) for which nominal protection was fairly low with the exception of apparel whose nominal protection was 39 per cent.

The remaining sectors (16 to 19) had a nominal protection higher than 25 per cent. These sectors mainly produce consumption durables (electro-domestic apparatus in sector 17 and passenger cars in sector 18, a.o.) and capital goods. The comparatively low nominal protection of the capital goods does not become clear in the present classification due to their aggregation with consumption durables.

The intrasector standard deviation of nominal protection is indicated in the second column of Table 9.3. It represents the dispersion of nominal protection between products within the sectors. In most cases it is fairly large, which suggests that the precision of the calculations could be improved considerably by working at a higher level of disaggregation.

However the decomposition of the intrasector variance into variances within and between branches, which is given in columns 3, 4 and 5 of the table, makes clear that a good deal of the variance already existed within the branches. Consequently, also at the branch level at which the effective-protection calculations were performed, nominal protection was far from homogeneous so that the assumption of uniform revaluation of input-output rows may have introduced biases in the results.

9.3   Effective Protection

9.3.1 The Input-Output Table

The input-output table used in the effective-protection calculations was obtained by updating the input-output table for 1975 elaborated by the Mexican Statistical Office.[6] The updating was performed with an improved RAS method along the lines described by Ten Kate in a previous updating exercise.[7] The input-output table for 1980 obtained in this way has the same activity classification as national accounts, that is, 72 branches are distinguished. Imports are registered in a non-competitive way, that is, in a row according to their economic destination, and domestic flows of goods and services are valued at producers' prices including indirect commodity taxes.

To convert the valuation of the table to basic prices more detailed information was required about indirect commodity taxation. As the national accounts only present global figures for indirect taxes net of subsidies, additional information was obtained in the Statistical Office which permitted splitting up the global figures into commodity taxes, non-commodity taxes, import taxes, export taxes and finally subsidies. Indirect taxes on mineral products were treated as if they were non-commodity taxes.

By assuming that the indirect commodity taxes were uniformly applicable to all input-output flows contained in the corresponding rows (except to the export flows), it was possible to establish an indirect-tax table equivalent to Table 5.5. With this the input-output table could be adjusted to a valuation at basic prices.

9.3.2 Indirect Taxes and Subsidies under Free Trade

In the project of the Ministry of Commerce, indirect taxes were treated according to the assumptions set out in Chapter 2, that is, they were assumed to persist under free trade on a specific basis.[8] This treatment, though essentially consistent if interpreted correctly, led to some specific results which easily lend themselves to

---

6. This input-output table was published as a part of the national accounts. See Secretaría de Programación y Presupuesto (1981).
7. See Ten Kate (1975).
8. See section 2.5.

misinterpretation.

The most important example is in branch 6, crude petroleum and natural gas, which is covered exclusively by the state-owned company PEMEX. As a result of the fact that both the internal accounting price for crude oil and the domestic distribution price for natural gas were far below international prices, the effective rate of protection reported by the Ministry of Commerce for that branch was strongly negative (-82 per cent). It should be explained that the company received at the same time an important positive protection in the form of monopoly access to the resources at a marginally low exploitation tax. As long as this exploitation tax is assumed to persist under free trade without any adjustment - as suggested in Chapter 2 - this positive protection is not taken into account and the strongly negative effective protection rate is not surprising.

It seems more realistic however to assume that as soon as the company is allowed to charge international prices for its output - which is the case under free trade - the exploitation taxes should be raised to levels reflecting the real value of the concessions. Unfortunately this value is extremely difficult to assess. It depends not only on international oil and gas prices but also on the probability of finding oil in the areas concerned and on the extraction costs once it is found.

Avoiding the quantification of such complicated factors but taking into account the positive protection implicit in the concessions, it was assumed that PEMEX should pay additional exploitation taxes on all its output at the rate of the export tax applicable to equivalent products on the export bill. By so doing the effective rate of protection to the branch was increased from -82 to -23 per cent, which is still fairly negative. Probably the assumption adopted for the value of the concessions was still on the conservative side.

Another exception to the rules set out in Chapter 2 is that of subsidies under free trade. As most subsidies granted were somehow linked with price support programme, they were considered to form part of price-control policies and thus of the system of protection. Consequently they were also suppressed under free trade.

9.3.3 Effective Protection by Sector

The effective-protection calculations were carried out at the 72 branch level of national accounts. For four input-output rows (agriculture, petroleum and gas, coffee processing and petroleum refining), additional information on the composition of the flows permitted a separate revaluation of some important entries. The remaining rows of the table were revalued with rowspecific deflators which were uniform within the rows. To arrive at the sector classification adopted in this chapter, the original and revalued tables were aggregated and the effective rates of protection presented in Table 9.4 were obtained by comparing value-added at protection prices from the aggregated original table with that at free-trade prices from the aggregated revalued table.

It should be mentioned that the nominal rates of protection of Table 9.4 do not coincide with those of Table 9.3. This is because th rates of Table 9.3 are applicable to total domestic sales while the rates of Table 9.4 refer to domestic final demand only. Apart from the non-uniform revaluation of some input-output rows, the aggregation of branches into sectors caused the differences.

The structure of effective protection shown in Table 9.4 is fairly similar to that of nominal protection. Differences are more outstanding in the case of effective protection but the ranking of sectors is almost the same. Only for sectors 2 and 11 are effective rates considerably less negative than nominal rates but this is due to the low internal accounting price for crude oil on the cost bill of the refinery branch. The most protected sectors are found in the modern manufacturing industries: rubber and plastic products with a high nominal protection on output and cheap petrochemical inputs and electrical apparatus and transport equipment also with high nominal protection on output and a much lower protection on its most important inputs.

Table 9.4 Effective Protection in Mexico in 1980
          (according to the original Balassa method)

Aggregate Sectors	Domestic at protection prices	Final Demand[*] at free-trade prices	Nominal Rates of Protection	Value Added at protection prices	at F.C.[*] at free-trade prices	Effective Rates of Protection
1. Agricult	225.7	201.6	12%	359.5	298.4	20%
2. Enerming	2.0	11.2	-82%	90.5	122.8	-26%
3. Othermin	2.1	2.2	-5%	56.8	54.3	5%
4. Meatdair	172.9	142.9	21%	31.4	16.0	96%
5. Grainmil	103.8	124.5	-17%	47.5	64.5	-26%
6. Oilsfeed	25.8	22.5	15%	20.9	13.9	50%
7. Othfoods	90.2	85.4	6%	70.0	58.7	19%
8. Bevtobac	104.6	128.2	-18%	49.8	70.2	-29%
9. Textleat	184.0	149.3	23%	120.3	88.1	37%
10. Woodpape	62.6	52.0	20%	84.0	59.7	41%
11. Petropro	22.3	65.5	-66%	23.4	34.1	-32%
12. Cheminds	70.3	61.4	14%	81.5	45.6	79%
13. Rubplast	23.6	14.9	59%	31.0	8.9	249%
14. Nomeminp	19.2	18.0	7%	53.6	40.6	32%
15. Basmetal	28.5	26.8	6%	59.4	42.5	40%
16. Metprods	103.1	80.0	29%	86.1	53.2	62%
17. Electrap	56.0	34.1	64%	37.1	12.5	197%
18. Transpeq	118.5	78.9	50%	61.0	22.6	170%
19. Otherman	32.3	23.9	35%	25.2	13.4	88%
20. Construc	575.6	575.6	0%	275.4	275.7	0%
21. Electrct	13.2	13.2	0%	47.0	17.6	167%
22. Commerce	616.4	616.4	0%	745.9	717.6	4%
23. Transprt	228.7	228.7	0%	263.5	202.3	30%
24. Otherser	989.1	989.1	0%	1060.1	1054.4	1%
Imports	163.9	163.9	-	463.9	463.9	-
Exports	423.3	423.3	-	-	-	-
Frgntradtxs	18.9	-	-	51.6	-	-
Othernettxs	122.7	122.7	-	303,0	604.6	-
Total	4599.3	4456.2	3%	4599.3	4456.2	3%

* Final-demand and value-added figures are given in billions of pesos.

It is interesting to observe the effective rates of the sectors
producing non-tradables under the assumption of the original Balassa
method. Almost all of them are positive, the rate of the electricity
sector even reaching 167 per cent. This positive protection stems from
two sources. In the first place there is the protection implicit in the
cheap energy inputs, which is particularly strong in the electricity and
transport sectors. Secondly the government subsidies should be
mentioned, which were important for the same sectors and for commerce.

Finally, note that the totals of the first and fourth columns of
Table 9.4 are the same;and those of the second and fifth columns
coincide also . This equivalence reflects the national accounting
identities (5.18a and b) at protection and at free-trade prices, as
discussed in section 5.4. Comparing the sums of columns 1 and 4 with
those of columns 2 and 5, it appears that under the assumption of the
original Balassa method average protection on the economy as a whole
resulted at only 3.2 per cent. This is mainly due to the weight of the
non-tradables whose nominal protection is zero in the present method.
Considering average nominal protection to the tradable part of domestic
final demand, the rate is considerably higher at 9.6 per cent. Average
effective protection to the sectors producing tradables is still higher
(24 per cent), but this percentage is brought down by an average
effective rate to the non-tradables of 5.5 per cent and a negative rate
to the government of -41.4 per cent due to the tax revenues forgone and
the subsidies granted under the assumptions of subsection 9.3.2.

9.3.4 Treatment of the Non-Tradables

The effective rates of subsection 9.3.3 are based upon the assumption of no price response of the non-tradables. There it is argued
that this assumption brings the average protection down from 9.6 per
cent for the tradable part to 3.2 per cent for the economy as a whole.
In the present sub-section alternative treatments of the non-tradables
are dealt with. In Table 9.5 the effective rates according to the
original and modified Balassa, Scott and Corden methods are presented.
In the modified Balassa method where effective protection of the sectors
producing non-tradables is assumed to be zero, the nominal protection of
the non-tradables is even lower than in the original method. In
particular the nominal rates for electricity and transport result

strongly negative. This reflects the fact that without government subsidies and with energy inputs at internationally competitive prices, electricity and transport would have to be considerably more expensive. As a result of the lower nominal protection of the non-tradables there is a slight increase in the effective rates of the tradables but average protection to the economy as a whole goes down to 1 per cent.

In the original Scott method nominal protection of the non-tradables is given a uniform level equal to the average nominal protection of the tradables which is 9.6 per cent. As a consequence the average protection to the economy as a whole also results in the same percentage. The higher nominal protection of the non-tradables leads to a reduction of the effective rates of the tradables but the effective rates of the non-tradables result considerably higher than in both Balassa methods.

In the modified Scott method it is the effective protection to the non-tradables that is supposed to be uniform. By putting it equal to 21.4 per cent, it becomes equal to the average effective rate of the sectors producing tradables. In comparison with the original Scott method, this implies an increase in the nominal rates of commerce and other services and a reduction in those of transport and electricity. On balance there is a slight increase in the effective rates of the tradables, but generally the effective rates of the tradables are hardly affected by the modification. The average protection to the economy as a whole increases from 9.6 to 10 per cent.

The effective rates according to the Corden methods add little to the observed structure. Due to the change from normal value-added to composite value-added in the denominator, the effective rates according to Corden are all lower in absolute value than the corresponding Balassa rates, as explained in section 6.3. In the Corden methods effective rates for the non-tradables do not make sense, consequently the average protection of the economy as a whole is not calculated.

Table 9.5 Effective Protection in Mexico in 1980
           under various treatments of the non-tradables

Aggregate Sectors	Balassa Original	Method Modified	Scott Original	Method Modified	Corden Original	Method Modified
1. Agricult	20%	22%	19%	20%	19%	20%
2. Enerming	-26%	-25%	-27%	-27%	-24%	-23%
3. Othermin	5%	6%	3%	4%	4%	6%
4. Meatdair	96%	110%	85%	87%	57%	65%
5. Grainmil	-26%	-25%	-27%	-27%	-23%	-21%
6. Oilsfeed	50%	59%	41%	42%	29%	35%
7. Othfoods	19%	23%	16%	16%	14%	17%
8. Bevtobac	-29%	-28%	-31%	-31%	-23%	-22%
9. Textleat	37%	42%	31%	32%	25%	29%
10. Woodpape	41%	47%	35%	35%	27%	31%
11. Petropro	-32%	-29%	-33%	-31%	-26%	-24%
12. Cheminds	79%	88%	71%	72%	52%	58%
13. Rubplast	249%	287%	211%	225%	123%	138%
14. Nomeminp	32%	39%	28%	31%	23%	29%
15. Basmetal	40%	49%	35%	38%	28%	34%
16. Metprods	62%	68%	55%	55%	42%	46%
17. Electrap	197%	224%	172%	171%	96%	107%
18. Transpeq	170%	193%	150%	150%	87%	98%
19. Otherman	88%	94%	83%	83%	66%	71%
20. Construc	0% (0%)*	0% (- 2%)	18% (10%)	21% (10%) -		-
21. Electrct	167% (0%)	0% (-38%)	244% (10%)	21% (-30%) -		-
22. Commerce	4% (0%)	0% (- 4%)	15% (10%)	21% (15%) -		-
23. Transprt	30% (0%)	0% (-15%)	50% (10%)	21% (-3%) -		-
24. Otherser	1% (0%)	0% (- 1%)	11% (10%)	21% (18%) -		-
Imports	0%	0%	0%	0%	-	-
Government	-41%	-41%	-41%	-41%	-	-
Average	3%	1%	10%	10%	-	-

* The assumed or implied nominal rates for the non-tradables are given
within parentheses.

Comparing the effective rates of the sectors producing tradables from one method to another, it appears that the difference between the original and the modified Balassa method is more noticeable than usual.[9] This is due to the relatively strong price distortions of electricity, commerce and transport induced by the government subsidies and the pricing policy for energy. This phenomenon suggests that, for purposes of project evaluation, proper attention should be given to the accounting ratios for energy and for the services intensive in the use of energy. The effective rates obtained with the remaining methods roughly follow the expectations set out in Chapter 6.

9.3.5 Decomposition of Effective Protection

From the policy-maker's point of view the most interesting results are in the decomposition of effective protection, where the intersector flows of subsidies (or penalties if negative) imposed by the system of protection become apparent.

The decomposition of effective protection according to the modified Balassa method is given in Table 9.6. The modified Balassa method has been chosen because in that method the implicit subsidies granted by the sectors producing non-tradables, such as electricity and transport, are most easily understood. To draw attention to the most important flows figures are rounded to billions of pesos. In this way all entries smaller than 500 million pesos are suppressed. As a consequence of this rounding the totals of rows and columns do not check exactly. There are differences up to two units.

To understand the table let us first consider the most important network of subsidies which is in the 'energy tree'. It starts with the flow of 222 billion pesos in the last input row (other net taxes) in the intersection with the column of energy mining. This represents the subsidy implicit in the concessions given to the exploration and extraction branch of PEMEX. In the second input row it can be seen how the exploration and extraction branch, in its turn, passes on the subsidy to the consumers of crude oil and natural gas. The major part of

9. In the numerical example of ch. 6, the differences are much smaller. Also in the previous study of the structure of protection in Mexico the effective rates according to the modified Balassa method hardly differ from those of the original method. See Ten Kate et al. (1980), app. B.

the subsidy goes to the refinery branch and the basic petrochemical industry both contained in sector 11. This subsidy was estimated at 219 billion pesos. Other sectors receiving considerable subsidies in this row are: basic metal industries, electricity, final demand and energy mining itself. The fact that total subsidies extended by energy mining exceed total net subsidies received is expressed by the negative effective protection of the sector of 31 billion pesos. However, as the subsidy implicit in the concessions was estimated roughly,[10] this negative protection should not be considered too significant.

The energy tree branches out further into the refinery branch contained in sector 11. In the corresponding row the subsidy received from the refinery branch is passed on and spread over practically all sectors of the economy. In decreasing order of importance, the receivers are: transport, final demand, construction, agriculture, commerce, other services, sector 11 itself, electricity and so on.

It should be noted that all sectors producing non-tradables receive large energy subsidies. According to the assumption of the modified Balassa method these subsidies, together with the direct government subsidies which were also important in these sectors, are passed on to the consumers of the non-tradables. This explains the positive flows over all rows 21 to 24.

Other important interindustrial transfers are detected in the row of agriculture in the intersection with the columns corresponding to the food and textile industries. Penalties are registered for meat and dairy products (sector 4) and grain milling, the latter being offset by equivalent government subsidies at the bottom of the table. As a result of the negative nominal protection for home-produced oilseeds, coffee, tobacco and cotton, among others, the transfers to the sectors receiving these products as inputs (sectors 6 to 9) were positive. Finally other transfers of some importance are found in the main diagonal, in the intersection of the chemical industries with the textile sector (synthetic fibres), in the construction sector and obviously in the final demand column, most of them being negative due to a positive nominal protection of the products interchanged.

10. See subsection 9.3.2.

Table 9.6 Decomposition of Effective Protection: Mexico, 1980
          according to the modified Balassa method (in billions of pesos)

Sources	1 Agcl	2 Enmn	3 Otmn	4 Mtdr	5 Grml	6 Osfd	7 Otfd	8 Bvtb	9 Txlt	10 Wdpp	11 Ptrp	12 Chem	13 Rbpl
Output:	44	-280	-3	33	-25	6	-	-23	43	30	-234	34	24
Inputs:													
1. Agricult	-4	-	-	-15	-7	1	3	1	1	-	-	-	-
2. Enerming	-	21	2	-	-	-	-	-	-	2	219	3	-
3. Othermin	-	-	-	-	-	-	-	-	-	-	-	-	-
4. Meatdair	-	-	-	-2	-	-	-	-	-1	-	-	-	-
5. Grainmil	1	-	-	-	3	-	-	-	-	-	-	-	-
6. Oilsfeed	-1	-	-	-	-	-1	-	-	-	-	-	-	-
7. Othfoods	-	-	-	-	-	-	4	1	-	-	-	-	-
8. Bevtobac	-	-	-	-	-	-	-	-	-	-	-	-	-
9. Textlthr	-	-	-	-	-	-	-	-	-6	-	-	-	-
10. Woodpapr	-	-	-	-	-	-	-	-	-	-7	-	-1	-
11. Petroprd	21	8	4	1	6	-	2	3	2	2	11	9	2
12. Cheminds	-1	-	-	-	-	-	-1	-	-5	-1	-	-5	-3
13. Rubplast	-1	-	-	-	-	-	-	-	-1	-	-	-1	-1
14. Nomeminp	-	-	-	-	-	-	-	-	-	-	-	-	-
15. Basmetal	-	-	-	-	-	-	-	-	-	-	-	-	-
16. Metprods	-1	-1	-	-	-	-	-1	-1	-	-	-	-	-
17. Electrap	-	-	-	-	-	-	-	-	-	-	-	-	-
18. Transpeq	-	-	-	-	-	-	-	-	-	-	-	-	-
19. Otherman	-	-	-	-	-	-	-	-	-	-	-	-	-
20. Construc	-	-	-	-	-	-	-	-	-	-	-	-	-
21. Electrct	1	-	1	-	1	-	1	-	1	1	-	1	-
22. Commerce	1	-	-	-	-	-	-	-	1	1	-	1	-
23. Transprt	1	1	-	1	-	-	1	1	1	1	1	1	-
24. Otherser	-	-	-	-	-	-	-	-	-	-	-	-	-
Frgntradtxs	-1	-1	-	-	-1	-1	-1	-	-	-1	-7	-2	-1
Othernettxs	5	222	-	-	7	2	6	-	-	-	1	-	-
Effective Protection:	64	-31	3	17	-15	8	13	-19	36	27	-9	38	23

14 Nmmp	15 Basm	16 Metp	17 Elca	18 Treq	19 Othm	20 Cnst	21 Eltc	22 Cmce	23 Trpt	24 Otsr	Fin Dem	Total	Source
6	10	39	30	48	12	-9	-30	-36	-64	-17	51	-309	Output
-	-	-	-	-	-	-	-	-	-	-	-24	-44	Agricul
4	9	-	1	-	-	-	7	3	-	-	9	280	Enermin
-	2	-	-	-	-	-	-	-	-	-	-	3	Othermi
-	-	-	-	-	-	-	-	-	-	-	-30	-33	Meatdai
-	-	-	-	-	-	-	-	-	-	-	21	25	Grainmi
-	-	-	-	-	-	-	-	-	-	-	-3	-6	Oilsfee
-	-	-	-	-	-	-	-	-	-	-	-5	-	Othfood
-	-	-	-	-	-	-	-	-	-	-	24	23	Bevtoba
-	-	-	-	-	-	-	-	-	-	-1	-35	-43	Textlth
-1	-	-	-1	-	-	-5	-	-1	-	-2	-11	-30	Woodpap
5	1	2	-	1	2	22	10	12	53	11	43	234	Petropr
-1	-	-	-	-	-	-2	-	-1	-	-3	-9	-34	Chemind
-	-	-1	-1	-1	-	-2	-	-1	-3	-1	-9	-24	Rubplas
-	-	-	-	-	-	-4	-	-	-	-	-1	-6	Nomemin
-	-2	-2	-	-1	-	-2	-	-	-	-	-2	-10	Basmeta
-	-	-2	-1	-1	-	-4	-	-	-	-2	-23	-39	Metprod
-	-	-	-3	-	-	-1	-	-	-1	-1	-22	-30	Electra
-	-	-	-	-3	-	-	-	-	-2	-1	-40	-48	Transpe
-	-	-	-	-	-	-	-	-	-	-2	-8	-12	Otherma
-	-	-	-	-	-	-	-	-	-	-	9	9	Constru
1	2	1	-	-	-	1	-	3	1	4	8	30	Electro
-	-	1	-	-	-	1	-	3	1	4	8	30	Commerc
-	1	1	-	1	-	6	-	3	2	2	41	64	Transpr
-	-	-	-	-	-	-	-	1	-	6	8	18	Otherse
-	-2	-2	-	-4	-1	-1	-	-3	-1	-1	-19	-52	Fntrdtx
-	1	-	-	-	-	-	12	20	16	9	-	302	Othnttx
15	20	35	26	40	12	0	0	0	0	0	0	301	Effectiv Protctio

Other important interindustrial transfers are detected in the row of agriculture in the intersection with the columns corresponding to the food and textile industries. Penalties are registered for meat and dairy products (sector 4) and grain milling, the latter being offset by equivalent government subsidies at the bottom of the table. As a result of the negative nominal protection for home-produced oilseeds, coffee, tobacco and cotton, among others, the transfers to the sectors receiving these products as inputs (sectors 6 to 9) were positive. Finally other transfers of some importance are found in the main diagonal, in the intersection of the chemical industries with the textile sector (synthetic fibres), in the construction sector and obviously in the final demand column, most of them being negative due to a positive nominal protection of the products interchanged.

9.3.6 Exchange Rate Adjustment and Net Protection

During 1980 the exchange rate of the Mexican peso was practically stable at a level of about 23 pesos to the US dollar. There was a growing deficit on the current account of the balance of payments which in 1980 amounted to almost 7 billion dollars, that is, 3.6 per cent of GDP. The major part of this deficit was due to interest payments on foreign debt but the commodity balance also registered a negative balance of 3 billion dollars while the balance of services was in surplus.[11] In 1980 the deficit on current account could still be financed with long-term capital inflows. Thus, according to the definition given in Chapter 7 the balance of payments was in equilibrium.

After the events of 1982 it is evident that this equilibrium was not stable but in the opinion of the author only a small part of this instability was due to the commodity balance. In fact the balance of payments became more and more dominated by oil revenues on one hand and debt servicing on the other. As it is not intended here to evaluate Mexican policies with regard to foreign debt, the apparent equilibrium on the balance of payments in 1980 is respected and the exchange rate adjustment calculated in such a way that it corrects only for the deterioration of the balance of payments that would result from the

11. For the statistical information see the statistical appendix to the annual report of the Bank of Mexico, Banco de México (1981).

elimination of the system of protection.

The exchange rate adjustment used to calculate net effective protection is obtained with formula (7.11) of the purchasing-power approach under the assumption of the original Balassa method, that is, net nominal protection of the non-tradables was assumed zero. As observed earlier,[12] this leads to an adjustment of the exchange rate equal to the average nominal protection of the tradable part of domestic final demand, which is 9.6 per cent.

The net effective rates of protection obtained in this way are presented in Table 9.7. It can easily be verified that the relation between the net effective rates of this table and the ordinary effective rates according to the Scott method[13] is almost standard. The only disturbing factor is formed by the net indirect taxes which are particularly important in sector 2 (energy mining). As a consequence the net effective rate for this sector is -47 per cent as against -34 per cent predicted by the standard relation. However if the oil and gas concessions should be valued at international prices, the corresponding indirect taxes under free trade would follow the exchange rate adjustment and the net effective rate of sector 2 would increase from -47 to exactly -34 per cent.

Apart from this special case, the structure of protection is hardly affected by the exchange rate adjustment. Only the average level of protection to the economy as a whole is lowered. Whereas this average level of protection was positive for all versions presented (up to almost 10 per cent for the Scott methods), it becomes zero with the exchange rate adjustment applied here.

To establish the correspondence with identities (8.12) and (8.13), the export figures of Table 9.7 have been transferred from the final-demand columns to those of value-added. By doing so, the totals of columns 1, 2, 4 and 5 become equal. The equality of the sums of columns 1 and 2 represents the closure of the domestic-final-demand circuit, that of columns 4 and 5 the closure of the value-added circuit.

12. See subsection 8.2.2.
13. See Table 9.5.

Table 9.7 Net Effective Protection in Mexico in 1980

(exchange rate adjustment = 9.6 % ; original Balassa method)

Aggregate Sectors	Domestic Final Demand* at protection prices	at free-trade prices	Nominal Rates of Protection	Value-Added at protection prices	at F.C.* at free-trade prices	Effective Rates of Protection
1. Agricult	225.7	221.0	2%	359.5	330.8	9%
2. Enerming	2.0	12.3	-84%	90.5	170.8	-47%
3. Othermin	2.1	2.5	-14%	56.8	60.7	- 6%
4. Meatdair	172.9	156.6	10%	31.4	18.8	67%
5. Grainmil	103.8	136.5	-24%	47.5	71.9	-34%
6. Oilsfeed	25.8	24.6	5%	20.9	16.3	28%
7. Othfoods	90.2	93.6	-4%	70.0	66.6	5%
8. Bevtobac	104.6	140.5	-26%	49.8	79.3	-37%
9. Textleat	184.0	163.7	12%	120.3	100.9	19%
10. Woodpape	62.6	57.0	10%	84.0	68.7	22%
11. Petropro	22.3	71.9	-69%	23.4	38.6	-40%
12. Cheminds	70.3	67.4	4%	81.5	52.8	54%
13. Rubplast	23.6	16.3	45%	31.0	10.8	188%
14. Nomeminp	19.2	19.7	-3%	53.6	46.1	16%
15. Basmetal	28.5	29.4	-3%	59.4	48.6	22%
16. Metprods	103.1	87.7	18%	86.1	61.2	41%
17. Electrap	56.0	37.4	50%	37.1	15.1	145%
18. Transpeq	118.5	86.4	37%	61.0	27.1	125%
19. Otherman	32.3	26.2	23%	25.2	15.2	66%
20. Construc	575.6	575.6	0%	275.4	256.3	7%
21. Electrct	13.2	13.2	0%	47.0	15.2	210%
22. Commerce	616.4	616.4	0%	745.9	715.4	4%
23. Transprt	228.7	228.7	0%	263.5	193.2	36%
24. Otherser	989.1	989.1	0%	1060.1	1046.5	1%
Imports	163.9	179.7	-9%	463.9	508.5	- 9%
Exports	-	-	-	-423.3	-464.0	- 9%
Frgntradtxs	18.9	-	-	51.6	-	-
Othernettxs	122.7	122.7	0%	303.0	604.6	-50%
Total	4176.1	4176.1	0%	4176.1	4176.1	0%

* Final-demand and value-added figures are given in billions of pesos.

Considering the value-added circuit, it is observed that the most important net donors of subsidies were: the government, mainly due to the indirect taxes forgone under the assumptions made, and the energy mining sector. Following in importance are the sectors: beverages and tobacco products, grain milling, petroleum products, and finally other mining. All remaining sectors are net receivers of transfers. For the sectors producing the non-tradables, this is due to the assumption of the original Balassa method which assumes that they do not pass on the subsidies received from the energy sectors. From the sectors producing tradables the most important net receivers are transport equipment, chemical industries, metal products, electrical apparatus and rubber and plastic products. In absolute terms agriculture is also an important receiver although the net effective rate of this sector is small.

10 Summary

Conceptual Background

The concepts of nominal and effective protection are intended to measure the protection granted to domestic producers by foreign-trade regulations, such as import and export tariffs, subsidies, licences and quota regulations. Their definition is essentially based upon a comparison of two situations: the protection situation, that is, the existing situation with the considered foreign-trade regulations in force, and the free-trade situation, that is, the hypothetical situation which would be obtained should the foreign-trade regulations be abolished.

Foreign-trade regulations are normally closely linked with other elements of economic policy, and many of them cannot be eliminated without carrying out a number of simultaneous adjustments in related policy areas. With that in mind the system of protection of a country is defined as the set of all foreign-trade regulations complemented with those policy instruments which cannot feasibly be kept in force when the foreign-trade regulations are eliminated. The most important related policy instruments to be included in the system of protection are price control policies for tradable goods (including foreign exchange) and a part of the indirect-tax system. The free-trade situation can then be redefined as the situation which would exist if the system of protection was abolished but with all remaining elements of economic policy unchanged.

The estimation of free-trade values for the main economic variables, such as the levels of production by sector, consumption by goods, employment and so on , would be a difficult task. Fortunately no such extensive knowledge of the free-trade situation is required for the assessment of nominal and effective protection. In fact nominal and effective protection measure the strength of the pulls and pushes exercised by the system of protection upon production levels, not the extent to which these levels react. As a consequence the knowledge of free-trade quantities is of secondary importance but that of free-trade prices is indispensable. Fortunately the latter can be approximated in a much simpler way than free-trade values for quantity variables.

Generally, no attempts were made to estimate free-trade quantities. Instead the present study may be considered as a device for the valuation at free-trade prices of quantities taken from the protection situation.

Nominal Protection

Nominal protection measures the impact of the system of protection of a country upon domestic price levels. More specifically, the nominal rate of protection of a product is defined as the extent to which the price of that product received by domestic producers in reality, exceeds the price they would have received under free-trade conditions. It is recommended to work with basic prices, that is, net of trade and transport margins and also net of indirect commodity taxes, because such basic prices are the most adequate indicators of the real receipts of the producers.

To estimate the free-trade prices of the tradables three major assumptions must be made. First it is assumed that under free trade, competition between domestic and international markets eliminates all price differences not explained by trade, transport and similar margins. Secondly the prices in international markets are supposed to remain unaffected by the elimination of the protection system of the country under study. Thirdly an assumption is made regarding the exchange rate that would prevail in the free-trade situation.

The three assumptions together pave the way for the estimation of free-trade prices for tradable goods. The only missing link is a proper correction for trade, transport and other margins to bring the international price on the same footing as the basic price with which it is to be compared. Obviously the correction cannot be assessed without making some additional assumptions, but the resulting nominal rates of protection are less sensitive to these latter assumptions than to the three mentioned above.

For simplicity's sake, the free-trade exchange rate is often assumed to be equal to the one holding in the protection situation. If however the exchange rate is adjusted to the free-trade conditions, the resulting nominal protection is called net as against ordinary nominal protection obtained in the absence of such an adjustment. For traded goods, and if the adjustment does not cause changes in trade directions, there is a standard conversion from ordinary to net nominal rates.

Although nominal protection is defined in terms of prices it can equally well be defined in terms of value. By stating it in value terms, the definition can be transferred direct to baskets of heterogeneous goods. In this way, the nominal rate of protection of a basket of goods is defined as the extent to which the protection value of the basket exceeds its free-trade value.

Measuring Nominal Protection

For imported goods whose importation is only subject to import tariffs, ordinary nominal protection is supposed to be equal to the applicable tariff rate expressed in ad-valorem terms. Hence there is no need for price observation. The same holds true for exported goods whose exportation is only subject to export taxes (or subsidies). However when tradable goods happen to be non-traded in either of the two situations, or when trade directions switch on the elimination of the system of protection, tariffs may become redundant and nominal protection is usually overestimated (in absolute value) by the tariff rates. When foreign trade - apart from tariffs, subsidies and similar price measures - is also subject to quantitative restrictions, these may lead to larger price differences than those caused by the tariffs and the tariff rate will underestimate nominal protection. In either case nominal protection is not measured appropriately by tariff rates so that price comparisons can no longer be avoided.

Unfortunately price comparison is always a complicated matter. Prices differ for many other reasons than just the system of protection. Prices increase along the way from the producer to the consumer and there are many more factors which may cause additional differences, such as quality grades, seasonal variations and so on. Moreover it is usually extremely difficult to identify products in international markets (or transactions) with exactly the same specifications as those produced domestically.

For such reasons it would be unwise to have too high expectations of the precision that can be achieved with the measurement of nominal protection through price comparisons. Generally international price comparison is far more difficult than intertemporal price comparison for the elaboration of price indices. Product identification problems may

reduce the representativeness of the sample considerably and it often
becomes necessary to 'enrich' the sample of price comparisons carried
out at the priceable level with unit value comparisons at some generic
level of product specification.

To avoid price comparisons leading to nominal rates of protection
very far off the mark, it is useful to consider the trade character of
the product involved - that is, whether it is imported, exported or non-
traded - and the trade regulations applicable. This information taken
together allows the definition of a permitted interval for the nominal
rate of protection, which can be used as a filter to exclude spurious
price comparisons from the sample.

Effective Protection

Effective protection measures the impact of the system of
protection upon value-added per unit of production. More specifically,
the effective rate of protection of a productive activity is defined as
the extent to which the value added generated by that activity in the
protection situation exceeds the value added that would be generated
under free-trade conditions with the production of the same basket of
goods.

To estimate the value-added that would be obtained under free
trade, the following steps must be made: (i) the basket produced is
valued at free-trade prices using its nominal rate of protection, (ii)
the free-trade input structure is defined, usually by assuming that it
is equal to the input structure observed in the protection situation;
(iii) tradable inputs are valued at free-trade prices using their
nominal rates of protection; (iv) non-tradable inputs and indirect taxes
are valued at free-trade prices by any of the assumptions available, and
(v) value-added at free-trade prices is obtained as a residue.

Economy-wide calculations of effective protection can be performed
by converting the valuation of an input-output table from existing basic
prices to free-trade prices. To that end the above-mentioned revaluation
steps must be applied to the input-output flows. Such an approach to
effective protection is slightly different from the customary approach
in which effective rates of protection are formulated in terms of input-
output coefficients. Although essentially equivalent, it is suggested
that the revaluation approach presented in this study gives a better

insight into the underlying assumptions than the coefficient approach.

The revaluation approach provides an overall consistent input-output table valued at free-trade prices. By subtracting that table from the original table valued at protection prices, effective protection is decomposed into its different sources and the intersector transfers induced by the system of protection are made apparent. Moreover the new table permits a restatement of national accounting identities at free-trade prices. By comparing them with the corresponding indentities at protection prices it appears that average nominal protection on domestic final demand is equal to average effective protection to value-added including indirect taxation. In this sense protection becomes a closed circuit. That is, the extra value added generated by the productive sectors plus the extra taxes collected by the government are spent again on the more expensive domestic final demand.

Non-Tradable Goods and Services

Goods or services are said to be non-tradable if they cannot feasibly be traded between different countries. For example, buildings and haircuts are non-tradable. For the non-tradables there are neither tariffs nor international prices. Hence their free-trade prices cannot be estimated in the same way as tradable goods. They are usually fixed by assumption.

Four alternatives are considered. In the original Balassa method the free-trade prices of the non-tradables are assumed equal to their protection prices, that is, nominal protection of the non-tradables is assumed zero. In the modified Balassa method the value-added generated with the production of non-tradables is assumed unaffected by the elimination of the system of protection: that is, effective protection of the activities producing non-tradables is assumed zero. The original Scott method assumes that the prices of the non-tradables follow the average trend of the prices of the tradables when the system of protection is abolished: that is, nominal protection of the non-tradables is assumed uniform and equal to the average nominal protection of the tradables. Finally in the modified Scott method the assumption is that value-added generated with the production of non-tradables follows the average trend of value-added generated with the production of tradables: that is, effective protection to the sectors producing non-

tradables is assumed uniform and equal to the average effective
protection to sectors producing tradables.

All these methods lead to slightly different input-output tables at
free-trade prices and thus to slightly different effective rates of
protection. However, if the price distortions of the tradable inputs in
the production of the non-tradables provoked by the system of protection
are not too large, the difference in the results between one method and
another are small and it is questionable whether the modification is
worth the additional complications.

If the exchange rate is not adjusted to the free-trade conditions,
and particularly if average nominal protection to the tradable goods is
large, the Scott methods lead to somewhat more realistic results than
the Balassa methods. But if the exchange rate is adjusted the difference
between the Balassa and the Scott methods is very small and any of them
will do.

An entirely different way to treat the non-tradable inputs in
effective-protection calculations is owed to Corden. In his approach
non-tradable inputs are not revalued at free-trade prices but aggregated
with value-added. The effective rates of protection are then defined in
terms of the composite-value-added concept. There is also a modified
version of the approach in which only the direct and indirect value-
added content of the non-tradable inputs is aggregated with the value
added of the activity considered.

It is demonstrated that all non-tradable flows of an input-output
table can be decomposed into direct and indirect tradable inputs and
primary factor inputs. This makes possible a contraction of the input-
output table, in which the sectors producing non-tradables no longer
figure but the column and row totals of the remaining productive
sectors, final demand categories and primary factor inputs are equal to
those of the original table. Effective rates of protection according to
the modified Corden method can then be obtained by revaluation of the
contracted input-output table at free-trade prices.

Although the Corden methods may lead to effective rates notably
different from those obtained by the Balassa or Scott methods, these
differences are not to say that the Corden approach is more or less
realistic than the others. The differences lie in the subject of
protection. In the other methods the subjects of protection are the

activities producing the tradables; but in the Corden methods the same
protection is extended to these activities together with all their
backward linkages with the non-tradables. For that reason the effective
rates according to Corden are usually smaller in absolute value than the
rates obtained with the other methods.

Exchange Rate Adjustment and Net Protection

The free-trade exchange rate - that is, the exchange rate at which
the balance of payments would be in equilibrium under free-trade
conditions - may well be different from the one holding in the
protection situation. Thus the exchange rate adjustment may be
considered as a kind of nominal protective rate for foreign exchange. As
the nominal protective rate of goods, the exchange rate adjustment
cannot be estimated with a high degree of accuracy either.

Two different approaches to estimate exchange rate adjustments in
the protection context are discussed: the elasticity approach and the
purchasing-power approach. The elasticity approach is based upon price
elasticities of supply and demand. By varying the exchange rate the
total balance of domestic supply and demand for commodities can be
influenced so that the commodity balance can be brought to equilibrium
(or to a prefixed surplus or deficit) by choosing an adequate exchange
rate adjustment. In the purchasing-power approach the adjustment is
chosen in such a way that the purchasing power of the domestic currency
in the free-trade situation is equal to that in the protection
situation.

Although the purchasing-power parity approach to the adjustment of
exchange rates between the currencies of different countries has been
severely criticised, it is argued that such criticism applies to a
lesser degree to exchange rate adjustments in the protection context.

Another argument favouring the purchasing-power approach over the
elasticity approach is that no such tricky quantities as price
elasticities are required. Apart from that, it is shown that exchange
rate adjustments of the purchasing-power sort lead to net effective
rates of protection which have meaning themselves even if the adjustment
should fail to bring the balance of payments to equilibrium. In fact net
effective rates obtained in this way no longer express protection to
value-added in money terms but in terms of the purchasing power of

value-added.

There is also a standard relation for the conversion of effective protection from ordinary to net rates. It has exactly the same shape as the standard conversion for nominal protection but the conditions to be fulfilled are somewhat more stringent. Sources of departures from the standard rule are now: (i) non-standard conversion of nominal protection; (ii) non-tradable inputs and (iii) indirect taxation.

It is demonstrated that, provided nominal protection follows standard conversion, the assumptions of the free-trade valuation of non-tradable inputs and indirect taxes can be adjusted along with the exchange rate in such a way that the standard relation is enforced upon effective protection as well. By doing this, the original Balassa method with an exchange rate adjustment of the purchasing-power sort is shown to be equivalent to the original Scott method without adjustment.

Finally it is shown that average net nominal protection on domestic final demand obtained with the purchasing-power sort of adjustment is zero. As average nominal protection on domestic final demand is always equal to average effective protection on value-added, average net effective protection must also be zero. In other words the exchange rate adjustment of the purchasing-power sort splits up the closed protection circuit into two separate circuits: the nominal-protection circuit between the purchasers of domestic final demand and the effective-protection circuit between the productive sectors and the government. Each of these circuits is then closed in itself.

The Structure of Protection in Mexico in 1980.

A brief survey is given of Mexican import substitution and related policies since the Second World War, and the state of protection policies during the late seventies and the early eighties is described in some detail. Then the structure of protection in 1980 is presented distinguishing 24 sectors of economic activity, 19 of them producing tradables, the remaining 5 producing non-tradables.

The composition of the product sample on which nominal protection is measured is briefly stared. The resulting nominal protection still shows the structure typical for developing countries on the import substitution track, that is, low or negative protection to primary commodities, intermediate manufactures and most capital goods, moderate protection to non-durable consumption goods and strong protection to the consumption durables. What places Mexico in a position apart is the extremely negative protection to energy and many petroleum-derived intermediates, which seems a logical consequence of the abundance of crude oil and gas. As a result of this strongly negative nominal protection to energy, average ordinary nominal protection was fairly low in 1980: 9.6 per cent on the tradable part of domestic final demand.

As usual the structure of effective protection is very similar to that of nominal protection but more pronounced. The effective protection of the energy sector depends in a sensitive way upon the assumption of indirect taxation in that field, that is, on what is considered an appropriate compensation for the monopoly concessions granted to the state-owned oil company. The intersector transfers provoked by the system of protection which are particularly strong in the energy sector are explained, using the decomposition table for effective protection. Finally net effective protection calculated with an exchange rate adjustment of the purchasing-power sort is presented and the results are used to reveal the closure of the separate protection circuits.

References

Adelman, I. and S. Robinson (1977), <u>Income Distribution Policies in</u> <u>Developing Countries: A Case Study of Korea</u>, Stanford University Press.

Allen, R.G.D. (1975), <u>Index Numbers in Theory and Practice</u>, Macmillan, Edinburgh.

Balassa, B. (1964), 'The Purchasing Power Parity Doctrine: A Reappraisal', <u>Journal of Political Economy</u>, vol. 72, pp. 584-96.

Balassa, B. (1965), 'Tariff Protection in Industrial Countries: An Evaluation' <u>Journal of Political Economy</u>, vol. 73, pp. 573-94.

Balassa, B. (1971), <u>Measuring the Nominal Rate of Protection</u>, Internal Note, Development Research Center, World Bank, Washington, DC.

Balassa, B. and D.M. Schydlowsky (1968), 'Effective Tariffs, Domestic Cost of Foreign Exchange and the Equilibrium Exchange Rate', <u>Journal of Political Economy</u>, vol. 76, pp. 348-60.

Balassa, B, and associates (1971), <u>The Structure of Protection in</u> <u>Developing Countries</u>, Johns Hopkins, Baltimore.

Banco de México (1981), <u>Informe Anual 1980</u>, Mexico, January 1981.

Bhagwati, J.N. (1978), <u>Anatomy and Consequences of Exchange Control</u> <u>Regimes</u>, Ballinger, Cambridge, Massachusetts.

Bueno, G.M. (1972), 'La Estructura de la Protección Efectiva en México en 1960', <u>Demografía y Economía</u>, vol. VI, No. 2, El Colegio de México, Mexico.

Bulmer-Thomas, V. (1982), <u>Input-Output Analysis in Developing Countries</u>, John Wiley, Chichester.

Cassel, G. (1916), 'The Present Situation of the Foreign Exchanges', <u>Economic Journal</u>, vol. 26, pp. 62-5.

Connolly, M., and D. Taylor (1976), 'Adjustment to Devaluation with Money and Nontraded Goods', <u>Journal of International Economics</u>, vol. 6, pp. 289-98.

Corden, W.M. (1966), 'The Structure of a Tariff System and the Effective Protective Rate', <u>Journal of Political Economy</u>, vol. 74, pp. 221-37.

Corden, W.M. (1971), <u>The Theory of Protection</u>, Clarendon Press, Oxford.

Dorfman, R., P.A. Samuelson and R.M. Solow (1958), Linear Programming
    and Economic Analysis, McGraw Hill, New York.
Dornbusch, R. (1973), 'Devaluation, Money and Non-Traded Goods',
    American Economic Review, vol. 63, pp. 871-80.

Eichengreen, B.J. (1983), 'Effective Protection and Exchange Rate
    Determination', Journal of International Money and Finance, vol. 2,
    pp. 1-15.
Evans, H.D. (1972), A General Equilibrium Analysis of Protection, North-
    Holland, Amsterdam.

Frenkel, J.A. (1978), 'Purchasing Power Parity: Doctrinal Perspective
    and the Evidence from the 1920s', Journal of International
    Economics, vol. 8, pp. 169-92.

Johnson, H.G. (1966), 'A Model of Protection and the Exchange Rate',
    Review of Economic Studies, vol. 33, pp. 159-63.
Johnson, H.G. (1969), 'The Theory of Effective Protection and
    Preferences', Economica, vol. 36, pp. 119-38.

Kalamotousakis, G.J. (1978), 'Exchange Rates and Prices: Historical
    Evidence', Journal of International Economics, vol. 8, pp. 163-8.
Kol, J., and L.B.M. Mennes (1983), 'Two-Way Trade and Intra-Industry
    Trade', in P.K.M. Tharakan (ed.), Intra-Industry Trade: Empirical
    and Methodological Aspects, North-Holland, Amsterdam.
Koo, A.Y.C. (1971), 'An Index Number Approach to the Effective Rate of
    Protection', Metroeconomica, vol. 23, pp. 257-73.
Kravis, I.B., and R.E. Lipsey (1978), 'Price Behaviour in the Light of
    Balance of Payments Theories', Journal of International Economics,
    vol. 8, pp. 193-246.
Krueger, A.O. (1978), Liberalization Attempts and Consequences,
    Ballinger, Cambridge, Massachusetts.
Kuyvenhoven, A. (1978), Planning with the Semi-Input-Output Method,
    Martinus Nijhoff, Leiden.

Leith, C.J. (1971), 'Equivalence of Average Effective Tariff and Average
    Nominal Tariff', Journal of International Economics, vol. 1, pp.
    353-7.

Lewis, S.R., and S.E. Guisinger (1968), 'Measuring Protection in a
    Developing Country: The Case of Pakistan', Journal of Political
    Economy, vol. 76, pp. 1170-98.

Little, I.M.D., T. Scitovsky and M. Scott (1970), Industry and Trade in
    Some Developing Countries, Oxford University Press.

Little, I.M.D., and J.A. Mirrlees (1974), Project Appraisal and Planning
    for Developing Countries, Heinemann Educational Books, London.

McKinnon, R.I. (1980), 'Exchange Rate Instability, Trade Imbalances and
    Monetary Policies in Japan and the United States', in P.Oppenheimer
    (ed.), Issues in International Economics,Oriel, London.

Meade, J.E. (1955), 'The Theory of International Economic Policy', Trade
    and Welfare, vol. II, London.

Niehans, J. (1980), 'Purchasing Power Parity under Flexible Exchange
    Rates', in P . Oppenheimer (ed.), Issues in International
    Economics, Oriel, London.

Ray, A. (1973), 'Non-Traded Inputs-and Effective Protection: A General
    Equilibrium Analysis', Journal of International Economics, vol.3,
    pp. 245-58.

Secretaría de Programación y Presupuesto (1981), Coordinación General de
    los Servicios Nacionales de Estadística, Geografía e Informática,
    Sistema de Cuentas Nacionales de México, Mexico.

Secretaría de Programación y Presupuesto (1982), Coordinación General de
    los Servicios Nacionales de Estadística, Geografía e Informática,
    Sistema de Cuentas Nacionales de México, 1978-1980, Mexico.

Soligo, R. and J.J. Stern (1965), 'Tariff Protection, Import
    Substitution and Investment Efficiency', Pakistan Development
    Review, vol. 5, pp. 249-70.

Squire, L., and H.G. van der Tak (1975), Economic Analysis of Projects,
    Johns Hopkins, Baltimore.

Stone, R.S. (1970), Mathematical Models of the Economy and Other Essays, Chapman and Hall, London.

Suzuki, K. (1979), 'Nontraded Inputs, the Effective Rate of Protection and Gross Output Changes', Journal of International Economics, vol. 9, pp.411-15.

Symposium on Purchasing-Power Parity, in Journal of International Economics, May 1978.

Taylor, L. and F.J. Lysy (1979), 'Vanishing Income Redistributions: Keynesian Clues about Model Surprises in the Short Run', Journal of Development Economics, vol. 6, pp. 11-29.

Ten Kate, A. (1972), The Treatment of Non-Traded Goods in the Theory of Protection, Discussion Paper No. 20, Centre for Development Planning, Netherlands School of Economics, Rotterdam.

Ten Kate, A. (1975), 'Estimación del Cuadro de Insumo Producto de México para 1970, con Base en el Método RAS', Investigación Económica, vol. 34, pp. 239-74, Escuela Nacional de Economía, UNAM, Mexico.

Ten Kate, A. and R.B. Wallace (1977), 'La Protección Efectiva en México en 1970', Investigación Económica: Nueva Epoca, Vol. 1, pp. 205-64, Escuela Nacional de Economía, UNAM, Mexico.

Ten Kate, A., and R.B. Wallace (1980), Protection and Economic Development in Mexico, Gower, Farnborough.

Tinbergen J. (1966), 'Some Refinements of the Semi-Input-Output Method', Pakistan Development Review, vol.6, pp. 243-7.

United Nations (1973), Problems of Input-Output Tables and Analysis: Studies in Methods, Series F, No. 14, New York.

United Nations (1968), A System of National Accounts: Studies in Methods, Series F, No. 2, Rev. 3, New York.

Waarts, A., A. Ten Kate and R.B. Wallace (1976), 'La Protección Nominal en la Economía Mexicana: Su Medición para 1970', Investigación Económica, vol. 35, pp. 237-303, Escuela Nacional de Economía, UNAM, Mexico.

Author index

Adelman, I. 91
Allen, R.G.D. 46

Balassa, B. 3, 5, 11, 18, 21, 28,
    33, 48, 58, 63, 66-7, 93-5, 98, 100
    103-5, 107-12, 115, 118, 120, 122,
    127-133, 136, 142-7, 154, 167-178,
    183, 184, 186
Bhagwati, J.N. 58
Bueno, G.M. 154
Bulmer-Thomas, V. 69

Cassel, G. 131, 132
Connolly, M. 143
Corden, W.M. 3, 5, 11, 18, 20, 23,
    28, 57, 58, 66, 67, 99-105, 107,
    108, 115-120, 128, 130, 168-170, 183,
    184

Dorfman, R. 91
Dornbusch, R. 143

Eichengreen, B.J. 133
Evans, H.D. 91

Frenkel, J.A. 132

Guisinger, S.E. 19, 59, 99

Johnson, H.G. 127, 128, 133

Kalomotousakis, G.J. 131

Kol, J. 25
Koo, A.Y.C. 32
Kravis, I.B. 132
Krueger, A.O. 58
Kuyvenhoven, A. 67, 95, 98

Leith, C.J. 80
Lewis, S.R. 19, 59, 99
Lipsey, R.E. 132
Little, I.M.D. 96, 108
Lysy, F.J. 91

McKinnon, R.I. 136
Meade, J.E. 4, 57
Mennes, L.B.M. 25
Mirrlees, J.A. 108

Niehans, J. 137

Ray, A. 108
Robinson, S. 91

Samuelson, P.A. 91
Schydlowsky, D.M. 122, 127
    136
Scitovsky, T. 96
Scott, M. 3, 67, 96-8, 107-8,
    112-4, 120, 144, 146, 169,
    183, 186
Soligo, R. 18, 58
Solow, R.M. 91
Squire, L. 108

Stern, J.J.   16, 58

Stone, R.S.   91

Suzuki, K.   108

Taylor, D.   143

Taylor, L.   91

Ten Kate, A.   5, 92, 95, 154
    164, 171

Tinbergen, J.   95

Van der Tak, H.G.   108

Waarts, A.   154

Wallace, R.B.   5, 92, 154, 171

Walras, L.   91

Subject index

adjustment
  border tax   13
  exchange rate   23, 27-9, 38-42,
    121-46, 148, 149, 151, 152,
    175-7, 185, 186
  export tax rate   38-42
  free-trade price   139-42
  import tariff rate   38-42

Balassa method   3
  modified   66, 94-6, 103-5, 107-12
    118, 120, 147, 168-73, 183
  original   66, 85-8, 93, 94, 100,
    103, 107-10, 210, 142-7,
    167-71, 175-8, 183
basis (for indirect taxation)
  ad-valorem   13, 146, 147
  specific   13, 146, 164

contraction of input-output tables
    3, 101, 103, 107, 115-8, 184
Corden method   3, 169, 185
  modified   6, 101-5, 107,108, 115-20,
    147, 170
  original   99-101, 107, 108, 115, 120,
    170

devaluation   124-6

effective protection   1, 57-88
  average   4, 78, 79, 114, 148-51,
    166, 167, 182
  decomposition of   76, 77, 87, 88,
    104-6, 111, 118, 119, 171-4

  net   139-42, 148-51, 175-8
  ordinary   140, 141
  rate of   57-9
elasticity
- approach   4, 127-31, 135-7,
    148, 185
  demand   90, 127-9
  supply   90, 127-9
equilibrium
  balance of payments 121-4
    130, 131, 137, 138, 185
exchange rate   124, 126
  general   16, 91
  partial   128
export
- subsidy 8, 9, 15, 34-41,
    51, 53, 54, 60, 61, 65,
    83, 179
- tax
    8, 9, 12, 13, 15, 16, 35-9,
    42, 51-3, 55, 62, 64,
    69-71, 74, 82-8, 165

foreign-trade regime   1, 8-12
free trade   9-17, 179, 180
- conditions   2, 4, 15, 121, 180
- exchange rate   23, 27, 121-7,
    142, 185
- price   2, 3, 4, 14, 16, 20, 22-8,
    21
  quantities   17
-situation   2, 16, 17, 28, 29, 31
    35-41, 122, 139

indirect-tax system   10-4, 63, 64,
    69-71, 142, 146, 147

input-output
- approach 3, 5, 68-82, 182
- coefficients 69, 182
- table 69-71, 75-71, 81-6, 102

level of product specification
   generic 43-6, 49-51, 181
   priceable 21, 43, 44, 46-50, 158,
      161, 183

national accounting identities 78,
   88, 182
numerical examples 81-8, 109-20
nominal protection 1, 18-56
   average 4, 5, 29, 30, 78-80, 96,
      97, 148, 149, 169, 182
   implicit 19
   net 27-30, 140, 149, 150
   ordinary 27-30, 140
   rate of 20, 21, 27, 29-31
nominal tariff rate 18, 19, 33-5,
   42
non-standard conversion
- for effective protection 141, 142
- for nominal protection 28, 29
non-tradables 1, 3, 4, 66, 67, 72,
   73, 89-120, 132, 139, 140, 142-4,
   168-70, 183-5
non-tradedness 2, 25, 26, 28, 34-8,
   40-2, 52-4, 89, 90

overvaluation 125, 126, 133
   hypothetical 126
   real 126

perfect competition 22

premium to the licence holder 54,
   55, 67, 68, 73
price
   basic 21, 60, 61, 69, 84, 85,
      109, 146, 161
   buyers' 60
   comparison 3, 5, 19, 20, 33,
      43-54, 56, 158, 161, 182
- control 10, 14, 15, 155, 156, 165
   factor 59, 60
   f.o.b. export 24
- index number 31, 32, 46, 47
- measures 9
- (potential) export 24, 25, 35-40
   (potential) import 24, 25, 33
      35-40
   producers' 21, 60, 61, 69, 81, 82
   protection 20
principle (for indirect taxation)
   destination 12
   origin 12, 13
protection
- in Mexico 2, 4, 153-78, 186, 187
   net 4, 27-9, 139-52, 175-7, 185-7
- situation 8
   system of 10, 11
purchasing power
- approach 4, 127, 131-8, 148-52,
   175, 176, 187
- parity 131-8

quantitative restrictions 9, 19, 34
   43, 54, 55

Scott method 3, 107-9, 147, 184
  modified 67, 98, 99, 113, 114
    118, 120, 147, 168-70, 183
  original 67, 96, 97, 112, 113
    120, 147, 168-70, 183
semi-input-output method 95
small-country assumption 22, 23
standard conversion
- for effective protection 131, 143
- for nominal protection 28, 29, 140

tariff rate
  ad valorem 18, 33, 35, 36
  equivalent 34, 54, 55
  import 1, 18, 33, 35-41
taxes
  commodity 12, 15, 16, 61, 63,
    64, 83, 146, 147
  foreign-trade 12, 63, 78, 87
  non-commodity 13, 16, 61, 63, 64,
    83, 146, 147

trade
- character 25, 26, 28, 35-42, 13
- displacement factors 131, 148
- margins 21, 23-5, 61, 62, 68, 6
    82

u-measure 59, 60
uniform revaluation of input-outpu
- rows 66, 72, 163, 166

value-added
- at free trade prices 58, 62
    74-6
  composite 100, 103, 115-18
  in the protection situation 57,
    58, 60, 61
z-measure 59, 60